Descriptosaurus: Myths & Legends

Descriptosaurus: Myths & Legends builds on the vocabulary and descriptive phrases introduced in the original bestselling *Descriptosaurus* and, within the context of myths and legends, develops the structure and use of the words and phrases to promote colourful cinematic writing. This essential guide will enable children to take their writing to the next level, combine their descriptions of setting and character and show how the two interact. Children can then experiment with heroes, gods and supernatural beings to create a legendary story.

This new system also provides a contextualised alternative to grammar textbooks and will assist children in acquiring, understanding and applying the grammar they will need to improve their writing, both creative and technical.

Alison Wilcox has extensive teaching experience in schools in England and Scotland. Colleagues describe her methods as 'innovative and inspirational to even the most reluctant of writers'.

Descriptosaurus

Myths & Legends

Alison Wilcox

Routledge
Taylor & Francis Group

LONDON AND NEW YORK

First published 2016
by Routledge
2 Park Square, Milton Park, Abingdon, Oxon OX14 4RN

and by Routledge
711 Third Avenue, New York, NY 10017

Routledge is an imprint of the Taylor & Francis Group, an informa business

British Library Cataloguing in Publication Data
A catalogue record for this book is available from the British Library

Library of Congress Cataloging in Publication Data
Names: Wilcox, Alison, author.
Title: Descriptosaurus : myths and legends / Alison Wilcox.
Description: New York, NY : Routledge, 2016.
Identifiers: LCCN 2015031446| ISBN 9781138858701 (hbk.) |
ISBN 9781138858718 (pbk.) | ISBN 9781315717746 (ebk.)
Subjects: LCSH: Creative writing (Elementary education) |
Description (Rhetoric)—Study and teaching (Elementary) |
Vocabulary—Study and teaching (Elementary)
Classification: LCC LB1576 .W48759 2016 | DDC 372.62/3—dc23
LC record available at http://lccn.loc.gov/2015031446

ISBN: 978-1-138-85870-1 (hbk)
ISBN: 978-1-138-85871-8 (pbk)
ISBN: 978-1-315-71774-6 (ebk)

Typeset in Myriad Pro
by Keystroke, Station Road, Codsall, Wolverhampton

Printed and bound in Great Britain by
TJ International Ltd, Padstow, Cornwall

Contents

Appendix   231

Acknowledgements

My name might be on the front cover, but to complete this book took the help and support of a great many people. Without the unerring belief and support of my family and friends, I might never have reached the finishing line. Thanks to Andrew, Robert and Kitty for their patience and understanding; to my loyal black labradors, Alfie and Monty; to my wonderful parents, Ann and John, and to my friends, Gail and Jinny.

Bruce Roberts at Routledge has been the mastermind behind the *Descriptosaurus* series, and as always, I owe him an immense gratitude for his wise words, guidance and support. Sarah Richardson's efforts have been tireless and I am extremely grateful for her input and support.

Maggie Lindsey-Jones and her team at Keystroke have been exceptional.

The work of the National Literacy Trust is absolutely essential in helping to raise standards in literacy and their involvement was vital in creating the momentum to get the project started.

To Katie and Tom. I hope you enjoy reading about your adventures!

Introduction

BACKGROUND

When I first decided to write *Descriptosaurus* it was because my experience of teaching creative writing to children had revealed that many had great imaginations and lots of ideas, but did not have the descriptive vocabulary to communicate these effectively. This was partly due to a lack of reading or a passive involvement with a text so that the techniques and vocabulary were not absorbed. I have been delighted with the response to the original work and have seen many fabulous examples of descriptive writing.

After writing *Descriptosaurus*, I returned to the classroom to conduct further research on different ways to use the resource. It became evident that one of the weaknesses in children's texts was the way they connected their writing. Often the pace of their writing was dramatically slowed by lengthy, unnecessary detail because they didn't have the vocabulary to move the story on to another scene. I also found that displaying the text on the whiteboard and modelling the process was extremely effective. This was why the second edition included a CD and a section on connectives and adverbs.

NATIONAL LITERACY TRUST – DESCRIPTIVE WRITING COMPETITION

In 2013, I collaborated with the National Literacy Trust on a descriptive writing competition. I was astounded by the response and the quality of the entries. I think that too much attention is given to the apparent decreasing standards in schools, particularly in literacy, and not enough media attention given to the outstanding young writers and teachers in our classrooms today. The work and support of the National Literacy Trust are vital in maintaining and improving these standards.

WHY WRITE *DESCRIPTOSAURUS: MYTHS & LEGENDS?*

As part of the process, the National Literacy Trust analysed the genres children chose in their descriptive pieces. It is important that children are given the opportunity to develop their interests and passions. To ensure that children are engaged and enthused with creative writing, it is vital that they are, where possible, given a choice. The four genres that stood out as by far the most popular were: ghost stories; adventure; fantasy; and myths and legends, which is why we have decided to concentrate on these four areas.

The original research and model for *Descriptosaurus* arose as a result of teaching a unit on myths and legends. There was a wealth of resources to spark the pupils' creativity, and the texts were a treasure trove of excellent descriptive vocabulary and the use of figurative language. As the pupils' knowledge of the plots, themes, structures, characters and creatures became familiar, the ideas for using the formula and stories to create their own myths and legends became more and more imaginative. However, it soon became clear that when tackling the written task, the pupils' imaginations were being stifled by a lack of descriptive vocabulary to transfer the images and scenes to paper. Giving the pupils a wealth of vocabulary and descriptive tools to draw from, not only improved the quality of their writing, but unleashed some formidable imaginations.

S/C-I-R: SETTING/CHARACTER, INTERACTION, REACTION

Often pupils' action scenes are just a list of various actions, with no description of the setting, other characters or emotions. I have seen excellent descriptions of settings, but the character(s) does not move (interact) through the setting. They are disjointed pieces of description. I have, therefore, been experimenting with a new system, which I have called S/C-I-R, which has resulted in cinematic writing of an exceptional standard.

The resulting work has described the setting, moved the character through the setting, and described their reactions to what they see or the events in which they are involved. A model of S/C-I-R is included at the beginning of each chapter.

CONTEXTUALISED GRAMMAR LEARNING

Another benefit of this system has been to provide a contextualised alternative to the prescriptive, repetitive focus on textbook grammar in response to the introduction of the SPAG tests. Taking a number of sentences or phrases for setting, interaction and reaction, combining them into a descriptive paragraph of a scene, and then experimenting with different ways of combining the sentences, openers and length is a very engaging way of learning about grammar and its impact on the flow, sense and expression. I have also noticed that the discussion that results from this experimentation has a dramatic impact on the quality of responses to comprehension tasks.

The exercise can be extended to changing tenses, including adverbs, or even using it to write a scene for a playscript. These exercises can be done as extended sessions, as part of the planning, or as warm-up exercises. They are also excellent for modelled and collaborative learning. Different focuses can be used. For example:

★ Giving the class three sentences all starting with pronouns, and setting them the challenge of using different ways to open their sentences.
★ Asking them to use the three sentences to produce a paragraph of five or more sentences.
★ Blending the sentences, but changing them into the first person and present tense.

PLANNING AND EDITING

The age-old problem of ineffective planning and cursory editing still remains. To aid in this process, I have included a section in the Appendix on the structure and planning of a myth and legend, breaking it down into manageable parts. A plot planning sheet is also included in the Appendix, as is a planning sheet to collect ideas about the hero's special object. Developing a habit of using a planning sheet to brainstorm ideas will, as we all know, greatly enhance the final piece of text. Hopefully, the structure of the planning sheets will also aid in the structure of the story.

To help with the development of strong characterisation, I have also included a planning sheet for a hero and a creature.

To combat cursory editing, planning sheets are provided for object, setting and suspense. If phrases and sentences are collected for Setting, Interaction and Reaction for each of the scenes, and the process of blending, altering, reducing, practised in warm-up activities, is used, hopefully the editing will become more focused and effective.

NON-FICTION

Myths and legends are already used in many schools as a focus for a lengthy unit, which includes many and varied non-fiction tasks. Other ideas could include:

★ Instruction leaflets for encountering certain mythological creatures, for example, a gorgon.
★ A 'Wanted' poster for Robin Hood.
★ Diary entries for events in the life of a 'legend' – for example, King Arthur.
★ A newspaper article about an event – for example, in the Trojan War.
★ A discursive piece on what qualities are required for a character to become a legend; what achievements they would need to accomplish.
★ A travel brochure for a trip to an exotic location.
★ A government warning notice about travelling to a 'dangerous location' featured in one of the myths or legends.
★ An information booklet about the Greek or other gods.
★ A design for a new mythological object.
★ A sales advert for the auction on eBay of a mythological object – for example, Thor's hammer; Hades' helmet; Hermes' sandals; King Arthur's sword.

I have had so much fun writing this book, it has been hard to stay focused on the brief, as I constantly found myself writing lengthy action scenes, which expanded into short stories. I hope all those who use *Descriptosaurus: Myths & Legends* enjoy using it as much as I enjoyed writing it.

Alison Wilcox

Key elements

HISTORY

Myths are the oldest of all story forms and are to be found in many different world cultures. They originate from a time when people relied on oral story-telling to explain natural events, to answer questions about origins and creation, about life and death, to teach important values and virtues, as well as to entertain. Many have cultural importance, as they are a source of knowledge about the way of life of ancient civilisations – their history, beliefs and values.

Legends are also a source of historical information about what people believed and the way they lived, but unlike myths, although they are not entirely true, they have a historical stimulus and are based on a real event, person or place. In legends, the focus is on the adventure plot rather than the message.

There are many different types of myths, but *hero myths* are most like legends, and this book is, therefore, based on hero myths. For example, in the tales from ancient Greece, heroes had a central role – undertaking challenging quests and embarking on dangerous voyages. As with legends, they illustrate the importance of courage, with the hero battling against impossible odds, taking part in battles, tackling terrible creatures. They remain very popular today, and many modern-day fantasy stories have their roots in myths and legends – for example, the popular *Percy Jackson* series.

FORM OF ENTERTAINMENT

The success of myths and legends lies in their ability to educate, inform and entertain. They provide a sense of excitement, action and suspense, by transporting the reader into a new, exciting world where there are strange creatures and supernatural powers.

The tales often include:

- ★ A brave, heroic character with special powers, for whom the reader can root
- ★ An exciting undertaking involving physical danger (quest)
- ★ A special object or person that enables the hero to accomplish impossible challenges and quests
- ★ A journey to dangerous, exotic locations
- ★ A series of trials to overcome
- ★ Life or death stakes should the hero fail
- ★ A villain or creature to fight against
- ★ Many twists and turns
- ★ Fast pace, drama
- ★ Excitement and suspense
- ★ Rich, descriptive vocabulary
- ★ Action sequences – battles, fights, chase, capture
- ★ Last minute escapes and victory against all the odds.

A. THE HERO/HEROINE

A hero myth or legend needs a hero that the reader wants to follow, and who is capable of accomplishing awe-inspiring feats. (*For ease, I have referred to the hero (he), rather than alternating between hero/heroine.*) He should essentially be:

- ★ brave and clever and either have supernatural powers, or a special object, talent or assistance that gives him enhanced powers or skills.

It is also important that the hero develops or changes in some way as a result of his experiences.

Get to know your hero

- ★ Collect ideas of heroes from myths and legends you have read.
- ★ Decide on a name.
- ★ How old is he?
- ★ Think of details that could be used in your physical description, such as, face, eyes, voice, clothes or armour that reflect their personality, or skills.

★ Add a description of any distinctive features.
★ Who are his family and close friends?
★ What are his main interests?
★ What is his special talent/strength?
★ What is he most afraid of? What is his weakness? (This could be really important to the story, as you may want to make your hero face their worst fear or overcome their weakness as one of the obstacles they have to overcome.)
★ Does the hero or any of his family or friends have any secrets?
★ What has he got to gain by achieving the task, overcoming the challenge, or to lose by failing to do so?

Descriptions of heroes are not included in this book as the periods in which the myths or legends could be set range from ancient Greece and the Middle Ages to the modern day and it would be impossible to provide specific, detailed vocabulary and ideas in the limited space available.

B. THE VILLAIN

Opposites often occur in myths and legends, so if the hero is good and brave, he needs a villain to fight who is the opposite. The villain can be (a) human, (b) a creature, or (c) both, and is usually:

(a) selfish, greedy, power-crazy
(b) hideous, vicious.

As the villain could be a human or a creature, for ease, the term 'villain' (and 'he') has been used to refer to both.

It is possible that the enemy and hero share the same goal. It is their *motive* that is different. The creature may be controlled by a villain or simply terrorising an area, island, forest, mountain, cave, sea.

Get to know your villain/creature

★ Collect ideas of villains from myths or legends you have read.
★ Decide on a name(s).

★ Add a description of any distinctive features.
★ Where does he live? What type of place is it? Is it very secure, scary? Is it in an isolated location? How is it protected?
★ Who are his allies?
★ Does he have a special talent/object/weapons?
★ Does he have any secrets/weaknesses? How can he be defeated or destroyed?
★ What has he got to lose by the hero achieving the task?
★ What does he do to people who challenge him?

C. QUEST, CHALLENGE

The hero has a problem to solve. This could be:

(a) **A challenge** – surviving encounters with dangerous creatures.
(b) **A journey** – across a dangerous setting, for example, a sea, mountain, forest, underground.
(c) **A quest** – usually to do with someone or something in danger and involving:

★ Rescue: an object or person, e.g. a princess from a sea dragon; an imprisoned king;
★ Recovery: e.g. a golden fleece, a crystal sword, Holy Grail;
★ Prevention: e.g. preventing any more children being sacrificed to a monster; preventing an evil king from robbing the poor.

Make sure there is a good reason for making the journey or being in the setting. The consequences of failure must be so severe that the reader is aware that there is no going back and that the hero will have to face the many obstacles and dangers along the way until he reaches the end.

D. A DANGEROUS JOURNEY

The hero battles for survival:

★ against the elements, such as a storm on land, sea, hurricanes, floods, fire and explosions, or hideous creatures, e.g. sea monsters that block his path across the sea; a nine-headed serpent that inhabits a mountain cave; a fire-breathing lion that prevents passage through a forest.

E. SINISTER, DANGEROUS SETTING

★ In faraway, exotic locations, such as desert islands; *or*
★ A forest, cave, ruined city, castle, mountain.

Setting in a myth or legend is where:

★ the action takes place;
★ the object or person being sought will be found;
★ the quest will be accomplished.

There may be a number of settings as the hero travels to his final destination, overcoming obstacles and evading the main villain. In a myth or legend, the hero has to overcome a number of obstacles, which may all occur in different settings until he reaches his ultimate challenge.

Key points

1. Decide why the setting is important to the story

(a) What features are there that will help the hero?
(b) What **barriers** are there to entering or escaping from the setting?
(c) What **obstacles** are there to retrieving the object or person that has been hidden/stored?

2. Think of words and phrases to help you build up the description of the setting

(a) Imagine you have a camera and move it around the location, then zoom in to pick up extra details. Make notes of interesting settings from myths and legends you have read.
(b) Make a note of important obstacles or items that will assist or impede the hero's victory.

3. Be descriptive

Use figurative language such as **similes** and **metaphors**. Some chapters have ideas for similes and metaphors included in the word section.

4. Use senses to bring the setting to life for your reader

As well as sight, think about what your character can:

★ hear, smell, touch, taste

5. To increase the tension, create a storm

Storms add atmosphere and danger to the story, can be used to indicate a supernatural or divine presence and are useful to introduce other senses, in addition to sight, to add tension, such as sounds, touch and smells. For example:

> As he touched the handle of the hammer, he felt the metal grow warm in his hand and lightning sparked along its length. Above him, a hole opened in the clouds – a swirling vortex of black and silver and an immense dazzling, guillotine blade of lightning streaked across the sky and flooded the land. Around him, the wind whirled up in strange clouds, flurrying and swirling, until it had grown to a thing of force and fury, crashing and howling, darkening the air with billowing clouds of dust.

Add detail and description to paint a picture in the reader's mind. Giving a setting an atmosphere is more than stating that, *It was dark*. For example, adding more descriptive detail could give you:

> The whole world suddenly seemed unnaturally dark, as if it had been drained of all light before the onset of a terrible storm. She looked up to see a gigantic bank of dark cloud that hadn't been there moments before.

F. SUSPENSE

Chapter 1: Hooks to build interest and tension includes a number of ideas and sentences on how to create suspense and give a hint to the reader of the danger to come, or that the danger is getting closer.

(a) Entering the danger zone – what's lurking in the cave, at the top of the mountain, behind the shattered pillars in the ruined city?

(b) Feeling of being followed/watched.

(c) Fear of discovery in a hiding place as footsteps/voices, hisses/growls get closer; branches snap nearby.

(d) Use of punctuation to add suspense:

> ★ Include a sentence(s) that holds back essential information from the reader until its ending.
>
> ★ Use colons, commas and repeated full stops to delay the revelation.

Examples:

Entering the cave, he stopped dead in his tracks.

She heard the shuffle of footsteps, the scrape of metal. Silence. A shadow loomed over her. She dropped to her knees. Silhouetted in the trees was . . .

(e) Build a sense of tension by:

> ★ Making frequent references to time (the 'ticking clock' effect):
>> ☆ Could he make it in time?
>> ☆ He searched desperately for a way out. Frantic now . . . time was running out.
>> ☆ The next few seconds unfolded in horrifying slow motion.
>> ☆ For fatal seconds, they stared, unable to think or move. And as they faltered, the jaws of the trap closed around them.
>
> ★ Varying the length of the words, sentences and paragraphs to increase the pace and tension:
>> ☆ Use short words, e.g. *at once*, rather than, *immediately*.
>> ☆ Place several short sentences consecutively: *She ducked. He lunged.*

☆ Include one- or two-word sentences. For example: *Oh no!* or *Coming closer. Too close.*
☆ When the action is fastest use partial sentences, e.g. *He had to get to his sword. Had to reach the ledge. He staggered, stumbled, scrambled. Five paces more. He lunged.*
☆ Use short paragraphs – some may be a single line.
☆ Include lots of **verbs** to convey action and create a fast pace. Use several verbs in a sentence.

G. OBSTACLES

Examples of obstacles the hero might have to face are:

★ Ground (muddy, icy, uneven)
★ Impenetrable forests, swamps, bogs
★ Sheer mountains, flooded caves, labyrinth of tunnels
★ Menacing, hideous creatures
★ Injuries sustained on the journey or inflicted by the villain.

H. EMOTION

Show how the hero reacts to events, setting, villain, challenges, etc. The basic rule is the same as in any other genre – **'SHOW NOT TELL'**.

(A) Reaction

Describing how a character reacts to events in the setting brings the scene to life for the reader and enables them to empathise with the character's situation and to root for the hero. For example:

He was terrified as he heard her demonic cackle . . . she had returned.

This **tells** the reader that the character is **terrified**, but does not **show** how the character **reacts** to the situation.

Instead describe:

- ★ How he is feeling inside using, for example, heart or pulse
- ★ Facial expressions
- ★ Eyes
- ★ Voice.

For example, the same situation could be expanded to describe the character's reaction to the demonic cackle.

An explosion of adrenalin surged through his body as he heard the demonic cackle . . . she had returned. He searched the shadows between the trees. Scrambling to his feet, he began to move. He glanced back and froze. She was right behind him.

The next few seconds unfolded in horrifying slow motion, as her black cloak spread, wings sprouted from her shoulders and her nose stretched into a sharp beak. Flapping her wings, she flew into the trees and circled above his head, transformed into a raven.

Note: The hero will experience many emotions during his adventure, but for the purposes of this book, the reactions for each section have been limited to mainly fear, anger and determination, as these are the common emotions that you would expect the hero to feel whilst he is overcoming his challenges and completing his quest.

(B) Interaction

To add a cinematic quality to your writing, it is essential that the action scenes include a description of the character's movements as he reacts to the events, to the villain, and moves through the setting. The character may:

- ★ be frozen to the spot
- ★ move nervously, cautiously, furtively
- ★ duck behind a tree
- ★ move quickly – jump, spin, leap, whirl, dash, sprint
- ★ frantically look for a way of escape
- ★ move forward to defend himself.

Apart from enabling the reader to visualise the characters' movements, their interaction is a signpost to the reader of the degree of danger and the closeness of the threat. For example:

She crouched on the ground. She was terrified of raising her head.

She darted and dodged around the pillars. Blundering and slipping on the gravel and stones, she ran for the wall, pushed off the ground, lunged for the ledge and frantically scrabbled for a grip to pull herself up. She had almost hauled herself over the top when her foot slipped and stones cascaded beneath her feet.

Part 1
The setting

1

Hooks to build interest and tension

Note: Apart from aiding the flow of your writing, this chapter can also be used to stimulate quick, brainstorming activities to get your creative juices flowing by asking the questions – Why? How? When? Where? Who? What happened? It is amazing how many stories can be created as a result of these quick activities.

OPENINGS

- ⋆ There was something strange about the hammer – she could feel it – sense something, a presence.
- ⋆ He would remember this moment later. He would remember the excitement about finding the spear. Then, everything was normal and he had been unaware of the approaching danger.
- ⋆ From that moment on, peace had been a brief, fragile thing doomed to shatter; the only question was when and where.
- ⋆ When he looked at the rippling reflection in the mirror, although he had no idea what it meant, he could sense that it was a warning. Warning him to get away while he still could.
- ⋆ He could sense the danger prickling down his spine. Every night since he had found the orb, he had dreamed of being pursued, chased by a menacing presence closing in around him, lurking in the background, but which he could never see. He didn't know how to put his unease into words as he didn't know what it was he feared.
- ⋆ She woke shivering with a sense of foreboding, a premonition of doom hanging over her, as if her dreams foreshadowed terrible events to come.

Frantically, she checked her neck to make sure that the locket was still there.

★ Sometimes, she wished she could just forget what she knew. Forget the day she had first learned about her powers.

★ He lay awake night after night, heart filled with dread; he knew he had to make the most difficult decision of his life.

★ It was days later that he would remember that moment.

★ They were nervous days while she waited for him to return. She knew that she had taken a step towards something sinister and there was no going back. Not now.

★ As he saw the air shimmering around the stone, he knew that the time had come, and he was terrified of what lay ahead.

★ *Nowhere was safe any more.*

★ He was shaken to the core by what he had just witnessed.

★ How different things would have been if she had never found the . . .

★ He shouldn't have followed them, or listened to their conversation. That was when everything started to go wrong. If he had known what would happen, he would have run the other way.

WARNING OF DANGER TO COME

★ He sensed that something was wrong here. Very wrong. Why had he come? Was it too late to turn back?

★ As she entered the forest, she looked up at the dark shadows between the trees and got the weirdest feeling; a feeling of unease and a sense of a threatening, malignant presence.

★ As soon as he had stepped into the city, an eerie sensation had enveloped him and would not go away. At night, in particular, he felt very uneasy. The feeling was getting stronger by the day. It was like the ruins were watching, waiting, biding their time.

★ As soon as he had entered the castle, he'd been fighting an underlying sense of panic and as night approached and the shadows lengthened, the castle suddenly felt full of dark secrets.

★ He couldn't shake off a sense of unease, a vague feeling that something was wrong, that he shouldn't have come.

★ *She was safe for now.*

★ On the fourth day of his journey, events took a different turn.

★ A horrible suspicion started building inside her.

★ There was something she couldn't quite put her finger on, something different, something not quite right.

★ A dreadful sense of misgiving began to creep over him, like the chill of a cold breeze.

★ He had all at once a dreadful, surging conviction of disaster hovering around the corner.

* She felt that she was caught in a maze without end, and round every corner lurked hideous monsters waiting to pounce.
* He had a sinking feeling in his stomach about what lay ahead. Something bad was about to happen and there was no way of escaping it.
* He still couldn't be sure that he was doing the right thing. There were too many things that could go horribly wrong.
* It was only just the beginning of a new chapter of dangers. All day she had been haunted by the feeling that something was coming; something of which she should be very afraid; something that was hunting her down.
* She tried to make sense of what she had heard. And as the truth dawned on her, she began to shake.
* He began to feel cold. Icy dread prickled his neck, warning him that danger was near.
* He had seen and heard enough to know that he was in grave danger.
* Out of nowhere, the hairs on his neck rose.
* Halfway through the forest everything went wrong.
* He had sensed something dark moving in the shadows, waiting for them, and now he knew what. There was no way of warning her what lay in wait; that she was escaping one nightmare and about to land in the middle of another.
* He had a feeling he was delivering himself into a trap, but nothing could have prepared him for what he met around the next corner.
* *All was still as death and dark as the grave.*
* It was very quiet. Too quiet!
* The night had been silent and now even the dawn chorus was still.
* When the breeze stopped, everything went very still and the forest became unnaturally quiet.
* Then there was silence. Even the wind seemed to have died down.
* It suddenly seemed frighteningly quiet. The air was charged with tension.
* There were all sorts of noises. They were probably nothing, but they reminded him that he had no right to be there.
* Every instinct in his body warned him that he was entering dangerous territory.
* *An owl hooted and swept by on silent white wings.*
* A scream from above caused his pulse to race. It was nothing more than a rook in the branches of a tree behind him.
* The wind howled. Great swirling gusts, relentless like an army of screaming banshees.
* *Shadows spread and lengthened. Their fear grew as night fell. Fear of the unknown. Fear of what lurked in the dark.*
* Twilight was closing in and she felt very uneasy.
* The last glowing embers of the fire slid into darkness.
* The shadows were now merging into one another, and the ground was being cloaked in the first shade of grey, heralding the night to come.
* It was dark with only flitting glimpses of the moon to keep them company.

- ★ *The mist came in with the tide, smothering everything like a giant fleece.*
- ★ He wandered like a ghost through the mist, guided by the murmuring of the river.
- ★ The night wind swept over them, whispering through the trees, shaping the mists into ghostly figures that flung flickering shadows in front of them.

THE TICKING CLOCK

- ★ His plan would buy him a few hours and nothing more.
- ★ When he opened his eyes, he guessed that a few hours must have passed. It was enough. It was time to make his move.
- ★ He counted the time by the pace of the shadows creeping slowly across the ground.
- ★ *The hours dragged past.*
- ★ The minutes seemed to crawl.
- ★ Tension mounted with every hour that passed.
- ★ The seconds ticked away, agonisingly slowly. It seemed to be taking forever.
- ★ An hour passed, and then another, and after a while . . .
- ★ In the long, agonising moments that followed . . .
- ★ It was late evening when it finally happened.
- ★ *The next few minutes were going to be vital.*
- ★ Time was of the essence.
- ★ He had less than a second to make a decision.
- ★ It was too late to turn back now.
- ★ There was no time to worry. No time to think. He had to act now. Time had run out.
- ★ She knew she didn't have long to act. It had to be soon.
- ★ He had only a second in which to act.
- ★ In the single instant that it took her to glance down . . .
- ★ The next seconds unfolded in horrifying slow motion.
- ★ *The clock was ticking down.*
- ★ She couldn't afford to wait any longer.
- ★ He could feel the seconds ticking away.
- ★ He knew they were running out of time. They might be too late.
- ★ If he had arrived too late, everything he had been through had been for nothing.
- ★ For fatal seconds, they stared, unable to think or move. And as they faltered, the jaws of the trap closed around them.
- ★ *They weren't going to make it in time.*
- ★ But he was too late, far too late.
- ★ He was too slow and one second too late before the gates slammed shut.

A DECISION/PLAN

- ✳ He knew his next move would be crucial. He ran through his options.
- ✳ The thirst to know as much as possible grew with each passing day.
- ✳ Over the next few days she concocted numerous plans and dismissed them all until suddenly all the details clicked into place.
- ✳ His rescue plan relied on stealth, cunning and a great deal of luck.
- ✳ He felt hopeless, but going back would be admitting defeat. It was time to fight back.
- ✳ It was an impossible task, but he refused to admit defeat.
- ✳ He was about to give up hope when . . .
- ✳ All the pieces were fitting together. She was beginning to form a plan.
- ✳ Suddenly, out of nowhere, he had an idea. He knew what he needed to do next and he knew he was taking a huge risk. But he had no other choice.
- ✳ It was then that she knew what she had to do. There was nothing left to lose.
- ✳ This was the moment he had been waiting for. He knew that the greatest trial of his life was approaching, but he had come too far to turn back now.
- ✳ She was convinced that they had reached yet another dead end. Suddenly, a light flashed in her head; a searchlight cutting through the dark maze. A jolt of memory as his words came flooding back to her.
- ✳ Somewhere, buried deep in her memory, she had a feeling she should know what she had to do next; that she had been given some clue.
- ✳ She felt there was an answer there – a vital piece of information she needed.
- ✳ Then came an incredible piece of luck.
- ✳ *It was all beginning to make sense at last.*
- ✳ With a jolt like an electric shock, he finally understood.
- ✳ In a split second, he realised what was happening.
- ✳ Just when he was thinking of giving up . . .

TOO CLOSE FOR COMFORT

- ✳ That had been close, too close. If he had been caught it would have all been over for him.
- ✳ She realised her mistake too late.
- ✳ The sound of footsteps behind her was all the warning she had.
- ✳ The footsteps were louder. Another roar . . . only seconds away.
- ✳ At that moment, she heard footsteps outside the door.
- ✳ Any second now, they would be discovered.
- ✳ The hooves seemed to be moving away from where he was concealed, but then, in a moment of utter terror, he heard voices behind him. They had dismounted and circled round and were now on his side of the track.
- ✳ The footsteps were growing louder and getting closer. He could hear the squeak of boot leather, the clank of a sword.

* *As he crouched in the ditch, he could hear the voices of the men close by in the shadows ahead of him.*
* Behind him, the soldiers were calling softly to each other.
* Suddenly, the breeze carried the murmur of her name.
* He was over halfway when the sound of voices alerted him to danger.
* He heard a voice whispering in the room, and he was aware that there was someone or something – standing very close to him.
* Then she heard something nearby, the slightest catch of breath.
* Nearer and nearer they came until he could smell their rancid breath.
* The squawks behind him grew louder and closer.
* *A noise close behind him made him turn.*
* It was a very soft thud, barely audible even in the absolute silence.
* He became aware of faint, muffled sounds of movement.
* Then he heard a sound – the quiet, stealthy sound of someone or something moving.
* A flicker of sound from the darkness caught her ear.
* Just then she heard something. She was on her feet immediately, crouching down. She heard another sound. The crack of a branch breaking, then another, and another. Someone or something was moving very fast through the forest towards them.
* He had already turned away and didn't notice the slight rise and fall of its chest, the brief twitching of its fingers.

DON'T DO IT!

* It was as if she was being pulled into something dark and dangerous by a hand she couldn't see, couldn't stop even if she wanted to.
* There was no reason why she was so desperate to go to the ruined city; she just knew she had to. It was as if she was being drawn by an invisible force.
* Despite her fear, she was seized with an urgent need to enter the cave.
* Something urged him on. Every nerve in his body screamed at him to get out. But before he knew what he was doing, his legs seemed to move of their own accord.
* She didn't want to look but she couldn't seem to stop herself.
* The cave summoned him like a dark, unblinking eye.
* Gripped by an urge to turn and run, he knew he couldn't. It was like an invisible thread was pulling him towards the mountain.

2
Objects

THE S/C-I-R STRUCTURE

He thrust the golden trident into the air. **He was not sure what he expected, so he was ready for anything.** He waited, scanning the sky, the sea, the surface of the waves. Suddenly, he caught sight of a dark mass on the horizon . . . a huge wave a long way off, but getting bigger and bigger, rising higher and higher as it thundered nearer, rising in an arch as it moved very fast towards him.

For a brief moment, the sight of the wave made his heart pound in his chest. He could not help looking into the dark, yawning entrance in the middle of the wave and wondering what he would find when he entered its gloomy depths.

As he watched the wave break into a roar of boiling foam, he braced himself. It swirled and seethed, crashed onto the rock. He was lifted off his feet like a rag doll and dragged under the surface of the water.

Tips

A magical object would help the hero complete his quest by giving him special powers to:

1. Seek guidance
2. Protect himself
3. Escape
4. Attack/destroy an enemy.

Examples of the skills he would need would be:

★ Speed
★ Strength
★ Enhanced hearing, sight
★ Ability to disappear – using an object that makes him invisible or enables him to transport himself to another location
★ Ability to see into the future
★ Ability to see what is happening in a different setting
★ Access to powerful weapons.

In modern spy and adventure stories, inventions – such as a pen that can shoot darts, or chewing gum that blows apart locks – assist heroes. In your myth or legend, any object can be turned into a magical item to assist the hero. For example:

★ Jewellery, watches, keys, clothing, shoes, sandals, belts, armour, helmets, weapons, sticks, gemstones, plates, cups, bowls, mirrors, scrolls, quills, books, boxes, feathers, scales, bones, twigs, stones, rope, musical instruments.

SECTION 1 – OBJECTS

WORDS

Nouns	**Poseidon**, Hermes, Hades, Thor, King Arthur
	Locket, necklace, pendant, lanyard, bracelet, ring, watch
	Crystal, gem, jewel, diamond, ruby, sapphire, emerald, pearls
	Key, lock, fire rod
	Box, chest, lid, tray, hinges
	Cover, sides, base, bottom, rim
	Book, manuscript, scroll, parchment, vellum
	Mirror, frame, surface, reflection
	Cloak, mantle, sandals, shoes
	Belt, buckle, plates, links
	Bowl, pestle, mortar, sickle

Hand, murderer, fingers, wax, candles

Rope, string, chain

Weapon, whip, staff, spear, shaft, blade, sword, pommel, hilt, hammer, mace, wand

Shapes, symbols, runes, patterns, words, images

Light, mist, glow, haze, fire, flames

Similes/ Metaphors

Like a huge, almond-shaped eye; rounded head like a shamrock; as strong as a steel-linked chain; like a sharp blade; like a huge, metal brick; fingers of fire; hung like a shimmering eye; pulsed like a heartbeat; wrapped around her arm like a serpent

Adjectives

Large, huge, enormous, small

Long, short, thin, thick

Heart-shaped, almond-shaped, rounded, curved

Blue, purple, green, red, ruby-red, golden, black

Silver, bronze, jewel-encrusted, steel, iron, metal

Wooden, oak, rosewood, leather, silk, enamel, glass, crystal

Cold, hot

Warped, battered, rusty

Glittering, shimmering

Sharp, serrated, double-edged

Mystical, mysterious, strange, eerie, enchanted

Verbs

Carved, engraved, etched, embedded, welded

Lined with, set, attached, protruded

Protected, covered, dipped in

Rose, hung, dangled

Creaked, lifted, slid, revealed

Lit, shone, glinted, pulsed, glowed, burned, blazed, sparkled, shimmered

Felt, tingled

Held, clutched, wrapped, raised, wielded, twirled, waved

Hissed, spat

Shrank

PHRASES – NOUNS AND ADJECTIVES

- ★ A heart-shaped locket
- ★ An enchanted, gold, jewel-encrusted bracelet
- ★ A diamond like a huge, almond-shaped eye
- ★ Glittering crystal of blue topaz
- ★ Large, ruby-red pommel-stone
- ★ Large fob watch
- ★ Small, iron key with a rounded head like a shamrock
- ★ White, silk cloak
- ★ Leather sandals
- ★ Metal belt
- ★ A large, leather belt with a golden buckle
- ★ A golden bowl
- ★ Small, golden sickle
- ★ Enamel dragons
- ★ Wooden box
- ★ Rusty hinges of the false bottom
- ★ A thick, leather-bound book
- ★ Mystical symbols and mysterious runes on the cover
- ★ Black mirror
- ★ Oak frame
- ★ Severed hand of a hanged murderer
- ★ Silver rope as strong as a steel-linked chain
- ★ Golden whip
- ★ Metal of the steel fire rod
- ★ Crooked, bronze staff about the size of a man
- ★ Long, wooden shaft
- ★ Double-edged, crystal sword of the Pendragon
- ★ Small dagger with a glass blade
- ★ Thin, sharp blade
- ★ *Bronze helmet*
- ★ Curved horns
- ★ *Like a huge, metal brick on the end of the hammer*
- ★ A metal plate like a sharp blade
- ★ Image of Thor
- ★ *Green mist*
- ★ Fingers of fire

PHRASES – VERBS

- ★ Carved with strange symbols
- ★ Carved with elaborate floral patterns

- ★ Sets of keys carved around the sides
- ★ Engraved around the base
- ★ Embedded with pearls and gold leaf
- ★ Outer circle was lined with weather symbols
- ★ Runic symbols etched in each metal plate
- ★ Words and symbols etched into the side
- ★ Curved plates of metal had been welded together as links
- ★ *Protected by a silver casing*
- ★ Bound in black leather
- ★ *Set in the pommel of the sword*
- ★ Set into the top of the hilt
- ★ Attached to the rim
- ★ *Rose from the bowl*
- ★ Slid down the side
- ★ Creaked as it slid open to reveal a tray containing . . .
- ★ Hung like a shimmering eye beside the . . .
- ★ *Glinted in the sun*
- ★ Lit up with an eerie glow
- ★ Began to pulse like a heartbeat
- ★ Began to glow
- ★ Glowed a brilliant blue
- ★ Burned with a cold tongue of blue fire
- ★ Blazed down the blade
- ★ Sparkled with a purple haze when held up to the light
- ★ Shone from the enormous buckle
- ★ Shimmered as he wrapped it around his shoulders
- ★ Cast a warped reflection into the hall
- ★ *Felt cold in his hand*
- ★ Tingled beneath his fingers
- ★ Knew that it could melt any lock
- ★ *Only his eyes were visible*
- ★ Covered his entire head
- ★ Covered the nose
- ★ Protruded from each side
- ★ *Dipped in wax*
- ★ Hissed and spat as he lit the fingers
- ★ *Towered above him*
- ★ Clutched his hammer
- ★ Wrapped around her arm like a serpent
- ★ Impossible for him to lift it, let alone wield it as a weapon
- ★ Started to shrink until it was small enough for him to hold in his hand
- ★ Hung it around his neck by the looped, leather lanyard
- ★ *Twirled the rosewood wand slowly in the air*
- ★ As she waved the wand, the runes carved around it . . .

SENTENCES

The large fob watch was protected by a silver casing and, instead of figures, the outer circle was lined with weather symbols.

Inside, he found a golden bowl with a small, golden sickle attached to the rim.

A green mist rose from the china bowl, slid down the side and over the dragons that had been engraved around the base.

The wooden box was embedded with pearls and gold leaf; the lid carved with elaborate floral patterns. The rusty hinges of the false bottom creaked as it slid open to reveal a tray containing . . .

The thick book was bound in black leather with mystical symbols and mysterious runes on the cover.

The crooked, bronze staff was about the size of a man, and towered above him.

She twirled the rosewood wand slowly in the air, and as she did so, the runes carved around it lit up with an eerie glow.

The black mirror, set in an oak frame, had sets of keys carved around the sides. It hung like a shimmering eye beside the door and cast a warped reflection into the hall.

The metal of the steel fire rod felt cold in his hand, but he knew that it could melt any lock.

The severed hand of a hanged murderer had been dipped in wax. Each finger hissed and spat as he lit them.

The golden whip wrapped around her arm like a serpent.

The double-edged, crystal sword of the Pendragon burnt with a blue fire.

A glittering crystal of blue topaz had been set in the pommel of the sword.

A large, red pommel-stone was set into the top of the hilt.

The small dagger with a glass blade sparkled with a purple haze when held up to the light.

The white silk of the cloak shimmered as he wrapped it around his shoulders.

Fingers of fire blazed down the blade so that the words and symbols etched into the side glowed.

The metal belt glinted in the sun as it shone on the curved plates of metal which had been welded together as links. In each plate runic symbols had been etched. The image of Thor clutching his hammer shone from the enormous buckle.

Only his eyes were visible in the bronze helmet which covered his entire head. A metal plate like a sharp blade covered the nose. Curved horns protruded from each side.

He stared at the huge metal brick on the end of the hammer. It would be impossible for him to lift it, let alone wield it as a weapon.

Slowly, the hammer started to shrink until it was small enough for him to hold in his hand. Taking hold of the looped, leather lanyard he lifted the hammer and hung it around his neck.

SECTION 2 – GUIDANCE

WORDS

Nouns	**Pouch**, wallet, satchel, scrip
	Book, manuscript, pages, scroll, seal
	Place, castle, trees, hills, mountains, cave, lake, waterfall, island, beach, lagoon
	Mirror, frame, glass, surface, reflection, outline, silhouette, scene
	Image, symbol, tree of life
	Light, mist, vapour, flames
	Ball, globe, orb
	Table, floor, mat, animal hide
	Herbs, dragon dust, salt, powder, liquid
	Pestle, mortar
	Scent, smell, dust, decay, incense
	Voice, whispers, crackle
	Breeze, gust, wind
Similes/ Metaphors	*Like a huge curtain of shimmering water*; *blazed like a candle; black seal like a bow and arrow; shimmering ribbon like a road*
Adjectives	**Huge**, heavy, small
	Smooth
	Leather, bronze, bronze-bound, silver
	White, sugar-white, turquoise, black
	Dry, husky, rasping
	Misty, shadowy
	Old, ancient, archaic

Verbs

Rose, sprang, floated, danced, released

Flicked, opened, turned, stopped, revealed

Ran, stretched, led

Cast, blazed, filled

Concentrated, blocked out, visualised, drawn into

Shimmered, rippled, misted, took shape, formed

Reached out, touched

Saw, glimpsed, watched

Heard, listened, whispered, hissed

Ground, sprinkled, mixed

Held, shook, tossed

Uncoiled, quivered, shuddered

PHRASES – NOUNS AND ADJECTIVES

- In front of him . . .
- From somewhere in front of them
- In the middle of the scroll
- From his leather pouch
- *Ring on his finger*
- Huge, bronze-bound book
- Silver rope
- Smooth bones slightly longer than a finger
- *A ball of light*
- Orbs of light
- Small globes of rainbow light
- *Surface of the glass*
- Smooth surface of the lake
- A reflection in the surface
- *A huge castle like a mailed fist*
- Trees, hills and mountains
- Waterfall like a huge curtain of shimmering silver
- Paradise island
- Sugar-white beach
- Brilliant turquoise lagoon
- Mouth of a cave
- *Symbol of the tree of life*
- Scent of incense
- Husky voice

PHRASES – VERBS

- *Sprang from her palm*
- Danced along his fingertips
- Floated over their heads
- Filled the room with light
- Danced through the air above their heads
- Came out of nowhere
- Sat on the table at his side
- *Blazed like a candle to light the way*
- Cast enough light for them to find their way
- *Took a handful of powder*
- Ground the herbs in the bronze mortar
- Cast salt mixed with dragon dust to summon . . .
- Flames hissed upwards
- Filled with white vapour
- *Saw only her reflection at first*
- Reached out and touched the frame
- Surface shimmered and rippled
- Misted up and suddenly . . .
- Concentrated on visualising the place
- Drawn into the surface of the mirror
- Where her reflection had been instead she saw . . .
- As the shadowy outlines began to take shape . . .
- Image started to form as a shadowy outline
- Slowly became clearer
- Could clearly see . . .
- Could hear sounds as the scene came to life
- Could see what was going on outside the . . .
- Unseen but watching their every movement
- Rippled as the breeze drifted through the air over it
- *When he touched the cover . . .*
- Stamped with a heavy, black seal like a bow and arrow
- Rose up from the scroll
- Pages flicked open with a dry crackle
- Pages stopped at a map of . . .
- Released the smell of dust and decay
- Whispered in an ancient language
- *Quivered under his feet as it uncoiled*
- Stretched into a shimmering ribbon like a road
- Ran from his feet far into the distance and over the hills
- *Held a handful of the bones between his palms and shook them*
- Tossed the bones onto the mat of animal hide

The ring on his finger blazed like a candle to light the way.

Flames danced along his fingertips casting enough light for them to find their way around the cavern.

He took a handful of the powder from his leather pouch, sprinkled it into the bronze mortar, and flames hissed upwards, filling the room with light.

As he walked in a circle, he cast salt mixed with dragon dust to summon the gnome.

A mist came out of nowhere, filling the room. From somewhere in front of them, a husky voice whispered in an ancient language.

At first, she saw only her reflection, then the surface rippled and where her reflection had been instead she saw the image of the ruined city.

He reached out and touched the frame, concentrating on visualising the place. The surface of the glass shimmered and rippled. Very gradually the image started to take shape from a shadowy outline until he could hear sounds and the scene came to life.

The glass misted up and suddenly he could see what was going on outside the cave, unseen but watching.

His eyes were drawn into the surface of the mirror as the shadowy outline began to take shape and he could clearly see a huge castle thrusting like a mailed fist out of a forest.

The surface of the lake rippled as the breeze drifted through the air over it. A reflection in the surface caught his attention.

The orb filled with white vapour.

Trees, hills and mountains rose up from the scroll, and in the middle was the mouth of a cave.

In front of him was a huge, bronze-bound book. When he touched the cover the pages flicked open with a dry crackle and released the smell of dust and decay. Eventually, they stopped at a map of the dwarf kingdom.

The manuscript was stamped with a heavy, black seal like a bow and arrow.

The silver rope quivered under his feet as it uncoiled and stretched into a shimmering ribbon like a road that ran from his feet far into the distance and over the hills.

The scent of incense was heavy in the air. The symbol of the tree of life sat on the table at his side. The smooth bones were slightly longer than a finger. He held a handful between his palms, shook them and then tossed them onto the mat of animal hide.

SECTION 3 – PROTECTION

WORDS	

Nouns	**Whistle**, horn, flute, harp, notes
	Lips, breath, throat
	Pole, staff
	Tube, stopper
	Belt, buckle
	Shield, barrier, energy, force
	Ripple, glow
	Dragon, wyvern, wings, scales
	Phoenix, eagle, feather
	Powder, water, blood, mixture, liquid, juice
	Fog, mist
	Strength, power, speed, sight
	Veins, nerves, sinews, muscles
	Features, details
	Wounds, cuts, bruises
Similes/ Metaphors	*Like powerful waves of energy; almost blinding speed; as though she was looking through a pair of high-powered binoculars*
Adjectives	**Bitter**, acidic, rancid
	Invisible, indistinct, blurred
	Tiny, small, thick, curved
	Deep, high, shrill, clear
	Silver, bronze, golden, blue, dark
	Wooden, acacia, wax, snake-skin
	Battered, crooked, scaly
Verbs	**Raised**, took, blew
	Carried, echoed
	Buckled, strapped on
	Opened, contained

Protected, warded off

Prayed, hoped

Flung up, threw, erected

Struck, clattered, sizzled

Swirled, rippled

Hid, obscured

Ground, dripped, stirred, mixed, drank, swallowed

Flowed, stung, scorched

Vibrated, surged, flooded

Moved, saw

Healed, disappeared, vanished

PHRASES – NOUNS AND ADJECTIVES

* In moments . . .
* *Tiny, silver whistle*
* Small, curved wooden horn
* *Dark, scaly acacia pole*
* Battered snake-skin tube with a thick wax stopper
* Scales of the wyvern's wings
* *Blue glow*
* Like powerful waves of energy

PHRASES – VERBS

* Took a deep breath
* Raised the . . . to her lips
* Blew a series of shrill notes that would carry to . . .
* Blew one clear note that echoed across the lake
* *Had no idea what it contained*
* Had to open the . . . only when he needed help
* Meant to ward off evil
* Prayed he would arrive in time
* *Flung up an invisible shield of blue energy*
* High and wide enough to protect them
* Clattered harmlessly against his invisible shield
* Sizzled into the barrier but got no further
* Glimpsed nothing more than a ripple in the air
* *Became obscured by a blanket of fog*

* Started swirling around her feet
* Gradually obscured her from view
* *As he buckled on the belt . . .*
* Felt something stirring inside him
* Rippled through his veins
* Set every nerve on fire
* Vibrated through every sinew
* Strength flooded his body
* *Ground the scales into powder and added some water*
* Let a few drops of blood fall into the water
* *Swirled the mixture with the phoenix feather*
* As she swallowed the juice . . .
* As the liquid flowed down her throat . . .
* Bitter juice stung her throat
* Could feel the liquid scorching through her veins
* After he had drunk the liquid . . .
* *Could move with almost blinding speed*
* Caught an arrow flashing towards him in mid-air
* *Had been granted the sight of an eagle*
* As though she was looking through a pair of high-powered binoculars
* Could see every feature, every detail of the rocks miles in the distance
* *Flowed to heal her . . .*
* Wounds appeared to be healed
* Cuts disappeared and the bruises vanished

SENTENCES

She put the tiny, silver whistle to her lips and blew a shrill note that would only carry to the Lady of the Lake.

She prayed he would arrive in time.

She took a deep breath, raised the small, curved wooden horn to her lips and blew one clear note that echoed across the lake.

He gripped the dark, scaly acacia pole that was meant to ward off evil.

He had been given a battered snake-skin tube with a thick wax stopper, but he had no idea what it contained, other than he was to open it when he needed help.

He flung up an invisible shield of blue energy high and wide enough to protect them. The spears clattered harmlessly against his invisible shield, sizzling into the barrier but going no further. The soldiers glimpsed nothing more than a ripple in the air.

The room was becoming obscured by a blanket of fog that started swirling around her feet and gradually obscured her from view.

He let a few drops of blood fall into the water, and swirled the mixture with the phoenix feather. After he had drunk the liquid, he could move with almost blinding speed. When an arrow flashed towards him, he caught it in mid-air.

She took the scales of the wyvern's wings, ground them into powder and added some water. As the liquid flowed down her throat, she could feel it surging through her veins, and when she opened her eyes it was as though she was looking through a pair of binoculars. She had been granted the sight of an eagle. She could see every feature, every detail of the rocks miles in the distance.

As he buckled on the belt, he felt something stirring inside him, like powerful waves rippling through his veins, setting every nerve on fire and vibrating through every sinew as strength flooded his body.

A blue glow consumed him, and in moments his wounds appeared to be healed – the cuts disappeared and the bruises vanished.

The juice was bitter and stung her throat as she swallowed it. She could feel it scorching through her veins as it flowed to heal her ribs.

SECTION 4 – ESCAPE

WORDS	
Nouns	**Air**, current, breeze, wind, whirlwind, vortex
	Circle, rectangle
	Agility, speed
	Shimmer, ripple, blur
	Phoenix, eagle, wing, feather
	Body, back, hands, legs, feet, hair
	Clothes, cloak, sandals, helmet
	Guards, sentries, warriors, creatures, monsters
	Door, mirror, stone, tunnel, portal, surface, ground
	Cliff, rocks, cracks, footholds
Similes/ Metaphors	*Like those of a huge eagle; as if he had been shot from a catapult; like vanishing behind a curtain of shimmering water; pulled back like rubber*
Adjectives	**Huge**, massive
	Red, black, grey, white

Leather, brick, stone

Round, oval

Impossible, incredible, unbelievable

Fuzzy, faint, indistinct, invisible

Slow, quick, fast

Outstretched

Verbs

Melted, dissolved

Sprang, grew, sprouted

Arched, stretched, fluttered, beat

Rose, lifted, catapulted, floated, flew

Flickered, rippled, swirled, gusted

Tugged, pulled

Spun, turned, circled, rotated

Streamed, poured, spilled

Held, clasped, squeezed

Climbed, slid, moved, walked

Swallowed, engulfed, vanished, disappeared

Found, discovered, realised

Shocked, disturbed, horrified

Dodged, ducked, evaded

PHRASES – NOUNS AND ADJECTIVES

- ★ All around her . . .
- ★ In front of him . . .
- ★ In a moment
- ★ All at once
- ★ *A current of air*
- ★ A red circle
- ★ A massive swirling rectangle of whirling air and then nothing
- ★ No more than a blur
- ★ With impossible agility
- ★ *Phoenix feather*
- ★ Two wings like those of a huge eagle
- ★ Leather sandals

PHRASES – VERBS

* ★ Could melt through locks
* ★ *Sprang from the neck of his cloak*
* ★ Fluttered from the sides of his sandals
* ★ *Arched his back and stretched*
* ★ Beat his wings
* ★ *Rose into the air*
* ★ Felt a force lift him up off the ground
* ★ Shot skywards as if he had been shot from a catapult
* ★ Felt like his whole body was floating
* ★ *As if the vortex was swallowing him up*
* ★ Air shimmered and then went black
* ★ Realised that his hands were fuzzy and indistinct
* ★ Could no longer see his own feet
* ★ Could see the trees through his body
* ★ Rippled as he vanished
* ★ As the cloak covered her . . .
* ★ Vanished behind a curtain of cascading water
* ★ Vanished in a faint shimmer
* ★ *Walked right past the guards without them noticing him*
* ★ Not one guard moved in his direction
* ★ *Stood arms outstretched*
* ★ Clasped her hands above her head
* ★ Breeze gusted around him
* ★ Swirled as if caught inside a slow whirlwind
* ★ Began to spin, faster and faster
* ★ Tugged at his hair
* ★ Tugged at his clothes
* ★ Cheeks pulled back like rubber
* ★ Eyes streamed
* ★ Lifted her off the ground
* ★ *Transformed into a portal door*
* ★ Would work as long as it was not cracked
* ★ Climbed into the mirror into the shadows beyond
* ★ *Solid brick surface rippled*
* ★ A tunnel appeared
* ★ Created a portal into which he disappeared
* ★ *Bounded down the cliff*
* ★ Found tiny footholds no bigger than coins
* ★ Dodged rocks that plunged towards him

SENTENCES

He shot skywards as if he had been shot from a catapult.

Taking the phoenix feather in his hand, he arched his back and stretched. Two wings, like those of a huge eagle, sprang from the neck of his cloak. He beat his wings, felt a force lift him up off the ground, and he rose into the air. His whole body felt like it was floating.

As she held up her hands, she realised that they were fuzzy and indistinct, and she could no longer see her own feet.

The air rippled as he vanished.

It was now possible to see the trees through his body. Then, all at once, he was gone.

She walked right past the guards and not one of them so much as moved in her direction.

The mist engulfed him as the air shimmered and then went black.

It was like vanishing behind a curtain of cascading water as the silvery haze swallowed her and she vanished in a faint shimmer.

A breeze gusted around him, tugging at his hair. His cheeks pulled back like rubber and his eyes streamed.

As she stood with her arms outstretched, all around her the trees swirled as if caught inside a slow whirlwind. A current of air lifted her off the ground.

Clasping her hands above her head, she began to spin, faster and faster until she was no more than a blur. Then she was gone.

The mirror had been transformed into a portal door. It would work as long as it was not cracked. He climbed into the mirror into the shadows beyond.

The solid brick surface rippled and a tunnel appeared ahead of him.

In front of him, a red circle appeared which grew larger, creating a portal into which he disappeared.

In front of him was a massive swirling rectangle of whirling air and then nothing.

She bounded down the cliff with impossible agility, finding tiny footholds no bigger than coins, dodging rocks that plunged towards her.

SECTION 5 – WEAPONS/ATTACK

WORDS

Nouns

Hand, fingers, fingertips

Bearer, holder, carrier

Sky, horizon, land, ground

Air, clouds, dust, wind, current, force, vortex

Bolt, ball, fork, flash, flare, blade

Lightning, electricity, thunder

Sparks, flames, fire, smoke

Water, spout, stream, wave, arch, crest, foam

Boat, ship, shore, cliffs

Fragments, shrapnel

Orb, wand, quill, spear, staff, trident, whip, sword, hammer, handle, tip

Cord, knots, wind

Beast, creature, monster

Similes/ Metaphors

Like an arrow-headed, pronged fork; like throwing a firework into the room; like tiny, jagged arrows of lightning; like heat from a furnace; struck him like a whip; like statues; like a rag doll; as if their legs had been cut out from under them

Adjectives

Huge, big, enormous, massive

Fast, quick

Pointed, sharp, razor-sharp

Red, blue, golden, bronze, white, white-hot

Icy, cold, warm, hot

Bright, brilliant, piercing, blinding

Curling, arching, spouting, swirling, boiling, seething, churning, foaming

Powerful, brutal, hideous, unstoppable

Still, motionless, immobile

Pungent, acrid, bitter

Deafening, ear-splitting, booming, thundering

Verbs	**Launched**, hurled, propelled
	Held, lifted, raised, thrust
	Twirled, flicked, pointed, stabbed, struck
	Tied, knotted, lashed
	Felt, touched, pressed
	Appeared, emerged
	Flew, shot, spilled, snaked, streaked
	Bubbled, thrashed, rose, ascended, spouted, burst, exploded
	Hit, slammed, sliced, pierced
	Radiated, emitted, filled, flooded
	Cracked, hissed
	Opened, parted, separated, divided
	Grew, whirled, flurried, swirled, billowed
	Darkened, dimmed
	Stood, froze, fell, crumpled, collapsed

PHRASES – NOUNS AND ADJECTIVES

* Above him . . .
* Severed hand of a hanged murderer
* Only he, as the bearer of the hand . . .
* A large spear, like an arrow-headed pronged fork
* Pointed quill
* *A bolt of white light*
* Bright, red bolts
* Piercing light
* An icy light
* Blue ball of electricity
* An electric current
* Swirling vortex of black and silver
* An immense dazzling, guillotine blade of lightning
* A wall of force
* *Ropes of flames*
* Tendrils of fire
* Pillars of smoke
* *A stream of water*
* Curling spout of water
* A huge wave a long way off

* Massive, hideous, unstoppable wall of water
* *Deafening crack*
* Frozen in time and motion like statues

PHRASES – VERBS

* Waited patiently, knowing he would not be affected
* Knew that soon everyone would be put into a deep sleep
* Would be asleep until he blew out the wax fingers
* *Raised his sword*
* Stabbed the bronze staff into the ground
* Held the staff upright
* Thrust the orb skyward
* Twirled the wand slowly in the air
* Flicked the whip
* As he touched the handle of the hammer . . .
* *Appeared in his hand*
* Flew from her hand
* Pointed it directly at . . .
* Threw it towards the beast
* Struck the ground at their feet
* *Shot from the tip*
* Shot from his hands into the sky
* Spilled out of . . .
* Snaked towards her fingertips
* *Appeared in the air*
* Streaked across the sky
* *Pointed the trident at the water*
* Water came to life
* Bubbled, thrashed and moved upwards
* Moved in a downward arc towards . . .
* *Like throwing a firework into the room*
* Threw up a shower of sparks
* Burst into flame
* Created a pungent cloud of smoke
* Exploded into razor-sharp fragments of blinding white light
* *Snapped against the wall*
* Flew across the cave
* Hit the walls like tiny jagged arrows of lightning
* Sliced through the air like shrapnel
* *Suddenly felt hot*
* Felt the metal grow warm in his hand
* Radiated from her like heat from a furnace

* Sparked along its length
* Cracked and hissed like lightning
* *Began to glow white-hot*
* Lit up with an icy flame
* Flooded the land
* Filled the room
* Flooded the room
* *Held the length of leather in his hand*
* Tied knots down its length
* As he finished tying the last knot . . .
* *Clouds parted*
* Wind grew stronger
* Grew to a thing of force and fury
* Whirled up in strange clouds, flurrying and swirling
* Darkened the air with billowing clouds of dust
* *Shuddered with a crack of thunder*
* Felt as if the ground beneath his feet . . .
* Being ripped apart
* *As he lifted the golden trident . . .*
* Could see a dark mass on the horizon
* Rose higher and higher as it thundered nearer
* Rose in a huge arch
* Moved very fast towards the ships
* Grew bigger and bigger
* Broke into a roar of boiling foam
* Swirled and seethed around the ships
* Pummelled and tossed the ships with its brutal power
* Threatened to bury the ships in a watery grave
* *Sharp enough to pierce a man's skin*
* Struck him like a whip
* *Stood stiff and still*
* Picked up the guard
* Lifted off his feet like a rag doll
* Threw the sentry bodily against the wall
* Blown across the room
* Fell to each side of the door
* Crumpled against the stone wall
* As if their legs had been cut out from under them
* *Split the stone in two*

SENTENCES

He waited patiently, knowing that soon everyone in the building would be put into a deep sleep that would last until he blew out the wax fingers. Only he, as the bearer of the hand, would not be affected.

A bolt of white light shot from the tip of his spear.

She twirled the wand slowly in the air and ropes of flames shot from the end. Within moments, pillars of smoke filled the room.

As he touched the ring, his hand suddenly felt hot.

She held the staff upright, stabbed it into the ground. It began to glow white-hot.

A stream of water appeared in the air, moving in a downward arc towards the encampment.

As he pointed the trident at the water, it came to life, bubbling and thrashing, and a curling spout of water moved upwards.

She felt as if an electric current had flown from her hand.

It was like throwing a firework into the room. It snapped against the wall and threw up a shower of sparks, creating a pungent cloud of smoke.

A blue ball of electricity appeared in his hand and he threw it towards the beast. It exploded into razor-sharp fragments of blinding white light that flew across the cave, hitting the beast like tiny barbed arrows of lightning.

Holding the length of leather in his hand, he carefully tied knots down its length. As he finished tying the last knot, the wind grew stronger, whirling up in strange clouds, flurrying and swirling, until it had grown to a thing of force and fury, darkening the air with billowing clouds of dust.

As he touched the handle of the hammer, he felt the metal grow warm in his hand and lightning sparked along its length. Above him, a hole opened in the clouds – a swirling vortex of black and silver – and an immense dazzling, guillotine blade of lightning streaked across the sky and flooded the land.

The quill was pointed and sharp enough to pierce a man's skin.

Bright blue bolts shot from her hands, striking the ground at their feet.

As he slammed the staff into the ground, it shuddered with a crack of thunder. It felt as if the ground beneath his feet was being ripped apart.

As he thrust it skywards, the orb lit up with an icy flame and a piercing light flooded the room.

As he lifted the golden trident, he could see a dark mass on the horizon . . . a huge wave a long way off, but getting bigger and bigger, rising higher and higher as it thundered nearer, rising in an arch as it moved very fast towards the ships.

It was massive, hideous, unstoppable. When it broke into a roar of boiling foam, it swirled and seethed around the ships, pummelling and tossing them with its brutal power, threatening to bury them in a watery grave.

There was a deafening crack as the stone split in two.

They were frozen in time and motion, like statues standing stiff and still.

He was lifted off his feet like a rag doll and blown across the room where he crumpled to the floor.

The soldiers fell to each side as if their legs had been cut out from under them.

A wall of force picked up the guard and threw him bodily against the wall.

3

The journey

Nouns	**Adventure**, journey, voyage, destination
	Mountains, slopes, top, summit
	Forest, woods, outlaws
	Ocean, waves, rivers, lakes, streams
	Miles, weeks, days, hours
	Day, night, moonlight, stars
	Settlements, stables, road, trail, path
	Footprints, camp fire, hoof prints, claw marks
Adjectives	**Long**, endless, difficult, challenging, dangerous, treacherous
	Dense, impenetrable, shadowy
Verbs	**Travelled**, journeyed, voyaged, headed
	Climbed, crossed, passed, faced with, avoided
	Trekked, trudged, tramped, plodded, stumbled, struggled, staggered, shuffled, scrambled
	Crept, hid, watched
	Guided, indicated
	Heard
	Entered, reached

PHRASES – NOUNS AND ADJECTIVES

* ⭑ Long journey
* ⭑ Difficult journey
* ⭑ All the way to . . .
* ⭑ Towards the shadowy north
* ⭑ At the end of the journey
* ⭑ *Miles and miles*
* ⭑ In the distance . . .
* ⭑ *Every day . . .*
* ⭑ For a week . . .
* ⭑ Hours before they . . .
* ⭑ For the next hour . . .
* ⭑ *Mostly by night*
* ⭑ Through the bitter cold of the night
* ⭑ Blackest depths of the night
* ⭑ *Full of dangerous outlaws*
* ⭑ Only occasional footprints or a camp fire
* ⭑ *A series of endless waves*
* ⭑ An ocean of rolling waves

PHRASES – VERBS

* ⭑ Going to be a long journey
* ⭑ Wherever she was going . . .
* ⭑ Would take them across . . . all the way to . . .
* ⭑ Headed towards the shadowy north
* ⭑ Travelled through . . .
* ⭑ Before they eventually reached their destination
* ⭑ *Would have to climb soaring mountains*
* ⭑ Find a way through dense, impenetrable forest
* ⭑ Cross treacherous ice fields
* ⭑ Pass an active volcano
* ⭑ Faced with new problems and challenges daily
* ⭑ *Journeyed mostly by night*
* ⭑ Guided only by the faint moonlight and the stars
* ⭑ Found a place to hide
* ⭑ Avoided any settlements and even the road
* ⭑ Crept into the woods
* ⭑ Hid under bushes and slept in stables
* ⭑ Slept under the trees
* ⭑ Kept watch, constantly alert for any sound or movement
* ⭑ Indicated that others had passed the same way

- *Moved up the trail*
- Reached the top
- Entered the forest
- *Trudged on in silence*
- Kept on walking
- Ran and walked, staggered and stumbled
- Pushed on relentlessly
- Sucked every ounce of energy out of them
- *Heard the sound of the river*
- Reached their destination
- *Fell to his knees*
- Buried his head in his hands
- Unable to believe he had actually made it

SENTENCES

They realised that somehow their old life had ended and a new one was about to begin. It was an adventure that would take them across seas and mountains all the way to the Isle of Avalon.

Wherever she was going it was going to be a long journey.

They knew they would have to find a way through a dense, impenetrable forest full of dangerous outlaws, pass an active volcano, and climb soaring mountains, before they eventually reached their destination.

His journey was difficult and every day he was faced with new problems and challenges. But he kept on walking, heading further towards the shadowy north that lured him on.

For three days, they rode past cascading waters toppling down the hills, up into the wooded foothills, then, finally, into the denser forest. As they rode, eagles and hawks soared overhead, following their progress.

For a week, she travelled on, journeying mostly through the bitter cold of the night, guided only by the faint moonlight and the stars. Where possible, she avoided any settlements, and even the road, unless she could be sure there was no one around.

They had travelled mainly through the blackest depths of the night, run and walked, stumbled and staggered, hidden in bushes, slept in stables, one of them always keeping watch, constantly alert for any sound or movement. Now, finally, they were at the end of the journey.

Kitty trudged on wearily for miles and miles, with only the occasional footprints or a camp fire to indicate that others had passed the same way. Finally, she heard the sound of the river.

Shouldering her quiver and bow, she moved up the trail, glancing up every so often to see how far she still had to climb before she reached the top.

He looked ahead and saw a series of endless waves stretching to the horizon. It seemed as if they were crossing an ocean of rolling waves, forever denied a sight of land.

They went miles and miles down the steep slope before they entered the forest.

He trudged on – silent, as exhaustion sucked every ounce of energy out of him, until, finally, he saw it in the distance. Falling to his knees, he buried his head in his hands, unable to believe he had actually made it.

4

Mountains

THE S/C-I-R STRUCTURE

She knew one thing for sure – this was the greatest trial of her life. Even though she had been trudging towards the summit, it never seemed to get any nearer. **Just staying on her feet was now a monumental task of sheer will-power and determination.** As she looked up, the mountain stretched high up towards the heavens, piled high with snow and carved by the gods into blade-like edges as sharp as scimitars.

A sheer rock-face rose up to her right, and cliffs dropped away to her left. She glanced back one more time and then continued to climb into the unknown. **Even though she knew she had taken a step towards something sinister and final, there was no going back now.**

Suddenly, there was a distant rumble like thunder, which grew louder, and the ground beneath her feet started to shake. Above her, stones cracked and exploded, sending fragments in every direction. It was as if the mountain itself was being shaken. She couldn't stay upright and was thrown violently backwards, teetering precariously on the edge of the path. For a dreadful moment she was hanging in the air, **her legs flailing and her eyes widening in fear** as she lunged with her right hand. **Her heart raced** as she felt her hand beginning to slip, her frozen fingers scrabbling as her body swung perilously over the drop. Her shoulders were burning. She was losing her grip. Her fingers slid towards the edge.

She thought they had made it, that their epic struggle was coming to an end. They were now tantalisingly close to the top of the mountain. The ghostly blanket of dark clouds that had covered the summit suddenly cleared and she saw what waited for them at the top. **Panic welled up inside her. She stared unblinking, as if in a trance and frozen to the spot.**

SECTION 1 – SETTING

WORDS

Nouns	**World**, country, land, horizon, scene, view
	Top, peak, summit
	Slope, climb, drop, ascent, descent
	Cliffs, rock-face, precipice, rocks, slabs, boulders, scree, rock-falls, landslides
	Pillars, arches, ridges, humps
	Crack, crevice, fissure
	Clouds, mist, fog, haze, shadows
	Streams, waterfalls
	Valley, gorge
	Fields, pastures, meadows, heather
	Path, route, road, trail
Similes/ Metaphors	***Like huge spearheads**; like menacing, black daggers; as sharp as scimitars; like enormous arrowheads; like the humps of a gigantic dinosaur; like a giant black shadow; like huge, pointed, black teeth; like a hungry mouth; like silver ribbons*
Adjectives	**Tall**, high, huge, soaring, enormous, massive, giant, gigantic, towering
	Amazing, majestic, magical, spectacular, magnificent, breath-taking, enchanting
	Rough, stony, rocky, uneven, sharp, pointed, rugged, jagged, craggy, shark-finned
	Steep, vertical, sheer
	Narrow, winding
	Dangerous, unstable, deadly, savage, harsh, hostile, lethal, perilous, threatening, ominous, menacing, treacherous
	Snow-capped, white-capped
	Black, dark, bleak, gloomy, inky, creepy, ghostly, shadowy, eerie, haunting, echoing
	Slippery, glistening, shimmering, glinting

Verbs	
	Rose, loomed, soared, towered, framed, surrounded
	Fell, dropped, plunged, plummeted
	Burst, thrust, thundered, erupted, pierced, slashed, gashed
	Carved, worn, sculpted, split, torn, ripped, cracked, shattered
	Scattered, blocked
	Sparkled, shimmered
	Covered, hidden, concealed, wrapped, enveloped, swathed, shrouded, shadowed
	Poured, gushed, hurtled

PHRASES – NOUNS AND ADJECTIVES

* From high up on the summit
* Somewhere below her
* Beyond the cliffs
* On the far side
* To the north
* Up to their right
* On their left
* *Land of the gods*
* Land of soaring mountains
* Majestic mountains
* Huge, snow-capped mountains
* Soaring summits
* Range of jagged, white-capped peaks
* Magical world of shimmering snow
* Spectacular views
* Magnificent cliffs
* Paths of shimmering pillars and arches
* *Lush, green meadows*
* Green valleys
* Carpet of purple heather
* *Cascading waterfalls*
* Streams like silver ribbons
* *Black, deadly mountains*
* Shadowy precipices, stony valleys
* Giant, eerie shadow of the huge, hostile mountains
* *Gloomy summit*
* Towering peaks
* *Craggy mountain*
* Great, jagged peaks

* Savage summits
* Bleak, perilous peaks
* Shark-finned ridges
* Enormous peaks like arrowheads
* Hunched shoulders of the craggy mountain
* *Steep, rocky slopes*
* Sheer rock-face
* Sheer, deadly slopes
* Bare, perilous slopes
* Steep, almost vertical ascent
* Sheer drop
* *Narrow, winding path*
* Inky black maze of steep, rugged paths
* Black boulders of jagged rock
* Shattered boulders and unstable rock-falls
* Great crevices
* *Veil of mist*
* Ghostly blanket of dark clouds
* *Deafening roar of churning water*

PHRASES – VERBS

* As they neared the cliffs . . .
* When she looked down . . .
* *Surrounded by breathtaking summits*
* Towered above the city
* Framed by the mountain's majestic peaks
* Filled the horizon
* *Rose to meet the sky*
* Soared above her
* Stretched towards the gods
* Had a spectacular view
* *Split, cracked and carved by the magic of the gods*
* Carved by the gods into blade-like edges
* *Thundered towards the sky*
* Pierced the sky above her
* Thrust sharply upwards
* Slashed by the stark, hostile mountains
* *Loomed ahead*
* Burst out of the forest
* Rose steeply to the top
* Loomed like a black beacon
* Erupted in sharp points

- *Fell away steeply to the left*
- Dropped into a black chasm
- *Snaked up the mountain*
- Glistened with damp
- Polished into dangerous, slippery slopes
- Shimmered in the haze
- Shattered by the gods into jagged blades
- *Blocked the path*
- Scattered everywhere as if there had been many landslides
- *Hurtled over the edge*
- Gushed out of a hole
- Poured out of the echoing gorges
- Plunged into the black depths below
- *Lost in wisps of cloud*
- Shrouded in mist
- Enveloped in thick storm clouds
- Covered by a veil of mist
- Covered by a ghostly blanket of dark clouds
- Could conceal an army of ambushers
- *Lay in wait*
- Warned them not to come any closer
- Waiting to crush him in their stony mouth

SENTENCES

The mountains seemed to stretch towards the gods, their summits lost in wisps of cloud.

He was surrounded by the soaring summits of the majestic mountains.

A magical world of shimmering snow towered above the city.

Split, cracked and carved by the magic of the gods, the rocks had created a path of shimmering pillars and arches.

The magnificent cliffs filled the horizon and beyond the cliffs a carpet of purple heather shimmered in the haze.

Through the hazy low cloud she could clearly see a range of jagged white-capped peaks.

Erupting out of the land, the savage summits of the mountains were like menacing, black daggers.

She gasped as she looked up at the hunched shoulders of the craggy mountain soaring above her. Its peaks rose and fell menacingly like the humps of a gigantic dinosaur.

To the north were mountains, with great jagged peaks thrusting sharply upwards, piled high with snow and carved by the gods into blade-like edges as sharp as scimitars.

The land was slashed by stark, hostile mountains, with peaks like enormous arrowheads warning them not to come any closer. This was the land of the gods!

It was a land of soaring mountains, savage summits, shadowy precipices and stony valleys. Rivers poured out of the echoing gorges to plunge into the black depths below.

The mountains loomed ahead like a giant, black shadow, their peaks like huge, pointed, black teeth waiting to crush him in their stony mouth.

The top of the mountain was covered by a ghostly blanket of dark clouds.

The mountain was a giant, eerie shadow covered by a veil of mist.

Shivering, he looked up at the gloomy summit lying in wait.

The bare, perilous slopes rose steeply to the top.

The steep path glistened with damp – polished by the gods into dangerous, slippery slopes.

A sheer rock-face rose up to their right and to their left cliffs dropped away into a dark abyss.

The dim light outlined the rims of the gorge; shadowy outcrops and crevices deep enough to conceal an army of ambushers.

As they neared the cliffs, the roar of the churning waters was deafening.

On the far side, the cliffs rose much higher. A river hurtled over the edge into the swirling mist below.

A narrow, winding road snaked up the mountain. It was a dangerous route; rocks were scattered everywhere, as if there had been many landslides.

SECTION 2 – INTERACTION

WORDS	

Nouns	**Climb**, ascent, drop, descent
	Top, peak, summit
	Ground, slope, path, edge, ledge
	Crack, split, hole, chasm
	Rock, rock-face, boulder, boulder field

Luck, fortune, events

Mist, thunder, cold, chill, wind, breeze, gust

Body, back, legs, knees, ankle, boots, feet, footing, arms, shoulders, hand, fingers, grip

Adjectives

Frozen, burning

Steep, sheer

Smooth, jagged

Bleak, wild, desolate

Small, fist-sized

Verbs

Climbed, trudged, scrambled, scrabbled, crawled

Grabbed, clung, dug, jammed, hauled, levered

Pulled, shoved, tugged, yanked

Hung, balanced, dangled, teetered

Edged, inched, wound, pressed

Jumped, leaped, lunged, swung

Shook, vibrated, cracked, exploded

Threw, flung

Slipped, slid, slithered

Swayed, flailed, buckled, slumped, fell, dropped, plummeted

PHRASES – NOUNS AND ADJECTIVES

- ⋆ On the final day of his ascent
- ⋆ For a dreadful moment
- ⋆ With his last ounce of strength
- ⋆ *Above him*
- ⋆ Across the top of the rock
- ⋆ Beneath his feet
- ⋆ Away from the towering, bleak summit
- ⋆ *A veil of mist*
- ⋆ Distant rumble like thunder
- ⋆ *Colder than ice*
- ⋆ Frozen fingers
- ⋆ Burning shoulders

PHRASES – VERBS

- Never seemed to get any nearer
- What she saw next changed things completely
- Began to turn against them
- Took a turn for the worse when . . .
- Happened in an instant
- *Slipped and slid on the rocks*
- Trudged towards the bleak summit
- Climbed slowly higher and higher
- *Crawled and scrambled up the steep slope*
- Linked arms and started to inch their way
- Wound their way around the rocks
- Edged along until they had . . .
- Pressed their backs firmly against the slope
- Tore their hands and knees on the jagged rocks
- Was aware that the edge was somewhere just ahead
- *Descended from the summit*
- Was hidden in the mist
- Blanketed the mountain
- The higher they climbed, the colder the air became
- *Clung to the side of the rock-face*
- Shoved, pulled, tugged at him ferociously
- *Climbed the boulder field*
- Jumped from one boulder to another
- Risked jarring an ankle with every leap
- *Leaped upwards*
- Grabbed the edge of the rock
- Lunged with her right hand
- Levered himself upwards
- Jammed his left arm into the crack
- Scrabbled with her fingers for a grip
- Took the full weight of her body
- *Balanced precariously*
- Swung out from the crack
- *Hauled himself onto the top*
- Tried pulling himself up in one motion
- *Dug in with his boots*
- Found a fist-sized hole in which she could jam her foot
- Brought his leg up
- *Would find no grip on the smooth face*
- Would be dangling over the sheer drop
- Would send him plummeting down
- *Lost his grip*
- Felt her hand beginning to slip

- ★ Scrabbled as her body swung perilously over the drop
- ★ Hung in the air, eyes widening in alarm, her legs flailing
- ★ *Lost her footing*
- ★ Began to slither towards the edge
- ★ Slithered down the jagged slopes
- ★ Teetered precariously on the edge of the path
- ★ *Dived towards her*
- ★ Grabbed her collar
- ★ Yanked her back
- ★ *As if the mountain itself was being shaken*
- ★ Grew louder and the ground started to shake
- ★ Cracked and exploded
- ★ Sent fragments in every direction
- ★ *Ducked behind a boulder*
- ★ Couldn't stay upright
- ★ Buckled under him
- ★ Slumped against the slope
- ★ *Thrown violently backwards by the force of the rock-slide*
- ★ Sent her sprawling to the ground
- ★ Fell as a fist-sized chunk of stone slammed into his side
- ★ *Bruised his arm*
- ★ Cracked her ribs

SENTENCES

He trudged towards the bleak summit that never seemed to get any nearer.

They had to wind their way around the rocks that protruded like grey teeth breaking through the earth.

They edged along until they had their backs pressed firmly against the slope.

Although his feet kept slipping and sliding on the rocks, he slowly climbed higher and higher.

Tearing their hands and knees on the jagged rocks, they crawled and scrambled up the steep slope.

They linked arms and started to inch their way across the top of the rock. They slowed down suddenly, aware that the edge was somewhere just ahead, hidden in the mist.

Fortune began to turn against them.

What she saw next changed things completely.

On the second day of his ascent, events took a turn for the worse when a veil of mist descended from the summit to blanket the mountain.

The higher they climbed, the colder the air became. He felt a chill surge through him, as he clung to the side of the rock-face with the wind shoving, pulling, tugging at him ferociously.

Then several things happened at once. Above him, stones cracked and exploded, sending fragments in every direction. He ducked behind a boulder, and nearly fell as a fist-sized chunk of stone slammed into his side, bruising his arm.

It was as if the mountain itself was being shaken. She couldn't stay upright. She was thrown violently backwards.

He climbed the boulder field, jumping from one boulder to another, risking jarring an ankle with every leap.

It all happened in an instant. There was a distant rumble like thunder, which grew louder, and the ground beneath his feet started to shake.

Leaping upwards, he grabbed the edge of the rock, and tried pulling himself up in one motion. Instead, he just hung there, his eyes widening in alarm, swaying slightly in the breeze. His shoulders were burning; he was losing his grip.

Kitty lost her footing, teetering precariously on the edge of the path for a moment. She began to slither towards the edge. Rob dived towards her, grabbed her collar, and yanked her back. As she collided into him, she sent them both sprawling to the ground.

She hauled herself up, finding a fist-sized hole in which she could jam her foot. Desperately, she scrabbled with her fingers for a grip.

Balancing precariously, he brought his leg up, then jammed his left arm into the crack which ran up the corner of the cliff.

He knew he would find no grip on the smooth face, that his feet would be dangling over the sheer drop, and that the slightest slip of his fingers would send him plummeting down.

She lunged with her right hand, and took the full weight of her body as she swung out from the crack.

Her heart raced as she felt her hand beginning to slip; her frozen fingers scrabbling as her body swung perilously over the drop.

For a dreadful moment, Tom watched her hanging in the air, her legs flailing and her eyes widening in fear as she reached out.

He dug in with his boots and levered himself upwards, and with his last ounce of strength, he hauled himself onto the top.

His legs buckled under him and he slumped against the slope.

They slithered down the jagged slopes, away from the towering, bleak summit looming above.

SECTION 3 – REACTION

Nouns	**Something**, force, phenomenon, presence
	Sense, instincts, feeling, thoughts, warning
	Task, struggle, trial, trap, survival, chances
	Anxiety, fear, shock wave, paralysis
	Willpower, determination, hope, optimism
	Breath, gasps, wheeze
	Pain, blood, wound, injury
	Body, hip, shoulder, arms, hands, legs, feet, step, head, forehead, mouth, voice
	Limbs, muscles, nerves, heart, lungs
Similes/ Metaphors	*Like a drum; like a clenched fist; like a dark fog; like a red-hot needle*
Adjectives	**Tingling**, prickling
	Painful, aching, sickening
	Dizzy, delirious, feverish
	Battered, bruised, exhausted, weakened
	Helpless, defenceless, powerless
	Strange, sinister, malevolent
	Vast, huge, epic, monumental
Verbs	**Worried**, bothered, concerned
	Felt, thought, wondered, considered, knew, realised, warned, urged, compelled
	Jolted, kick-started, ignited
	Staggered, faltered, slumped, stumbled, fell, toppled
	Glanced, peered, stared, fixed, glued, searched
	Breathed, gasped, shuddered, muttered, grumbled, groaned, moaned
	Crept, slithered, welled, pounded, hammered
	Tugged, pulled, gripped

Froze, stood, paused, hesitated

Lurked, loomed, waited, watched

Dripped, dropped, dribbled

PHRASES – NOUNS AND ADJECTIVES

* ★ Something about the mountain
* ★ Something sinister
* ★ A strange phenomenon
* ★ A menacing force
* ★ A shadowy presence
* ★ Tantalisingly close
* ★ Jaws of a trap
* ★ *Greatest trial of her life*
* ★ A small part of her
* ★ However slim his chances
* ★ *All around them*
* ★ Round every unseen corner
* ★ *When he eventually . . .*
* ★ For a few fatal seconds
* ★ *Again and again, the same thoughts*
* ★ Tingling sixth sense
* ★ Almost as if a voice inside his head . . .
* ★ *Every muscle in her body*
* ★ Every nerve in his body
* ★ Every step
* ★ With every ounce of strength
* ★ Sheer willpower and determination
* ★ *A trickle of blood*
* ★ Blistered feet
* ★ Bruised arm
* ★ *With his hands on his knees*
* ★ As if in a trance
* ★ *A low, painful wheeze*

PHRASES – VERBS

* ★ Bothered her
* ★ Made her wonder what powers could create . . .
* ★ What was he up against?
* ★ Knew one thing for sure
* ★ Was powerless to stop

- *Had come too far to turn back now*
- Would see it through together – whatever it took
- *Tugged at her*
- Drew her closer – like a fish on a line
- Had the strangest feeling of being called
- Screamed a warning, yet urged him to come
- *Glanced back one more time*
- No going back
- Never considered giving up
- Climbed into the unknown
- Knew they had all taken a step towards . . .
- *Kept running through his mind*
- Increased his sense of anxiety
- Felt as if he was caught in a maze without an end
- Felt like something was watching them
- Lurked, waiting to pounce
- Waited for them at the top
- *Turned but there was no one there*
- Made him look up
- Turned and froze
- Standing right above him was . . .
- *Just when he thought he was safe . . .*
- Thought it was safe until she saw . . .
- Changed things completely
- *Welled up inside her*
- Felt a familiar shiver
- Something was about to go terribly wrong
- *No time to ask questions*
- Only time to survive
- Knew his life hung by a thread
- Wondered what else would try to hinder him
- *Shrivelled with fear when he looked down*
- Saw how high up he was
- Pounded like a drum
- Panic was beginning to set in
- Crept over her
- Slithered around her like a dark fog
- Brought a damp chill
- Raced through his veins
- *It was as if time had stopped*
- Slithered to a halt
- Stood hands on hips, head bowed
- Shuddered and went rigid
- *Started to lose all memory of how to move her aching limbs*

- ✳ Felt battered and bruised, utterly exhausted
- ✳ Staying on her feet was a monumental task
- ✳ Weakened with every step
- ✳ Had reached her limit . . . couldn't go on . . . shutting down
- ✳ Slumped to the ground
- ✳ *Ached with the sickening pain*
- ✳ Screamed at him as the pain . . .
- ✳ Sprinkled red-hot needles across her arms and legs
- ✳ Gripped his shoulder like a clenched fist
- ✳ Sent a shock wave of pain through . . .
- ✳ Dripped down his forehead, and into his mouth
- ✳ *Knew that their epic struggle was coming to an end*
- ✳ Had nearly reached the top of the mountain
- ✳ *Moved her lips silently in prayer*
- ✳ Drew in a deep breath
- ✳ Came in painful gasps
- ✳ Gasped for each painful breath
- ✳ Blew out his breath hard to stop himself howling
- ✳ Started to become delirious
- ✳ Muttered, rambled, groaned
- ✳ *Stared unblinking above her*
- ✳ Stared, unable to think or move
- ✳ *Jolted him out of his paralysis*
- ✳ Kick-started his survival instincts
- ✳ Had to move. And soon
- ✳ Forced herself to keep calm . . . keep moving

SENTENCES

Something about the mountain bothered her.

He wondered what powers could create such a strange phenomenon. What was he up against?

He knew that however slim his chances, they were worth taking.

She knew one thing for sure – the greatest trial of her life was approaching. She had come too far to turn back now.

They would see it through together – whatever it took.

A small part of her wanted to turn back, but something larger tugged at her and she was powerless to stop.

He had the strangest feeling of being called, almost as if a voice inside his head was screaming a warning, yet urging him to come.

He glanced back one more time and then climbed into the unknown.

She knew they had all taken a step towards something sinister and final, and there was no going back.

She never considered giving up. Some force drew her closer – like a fish hooked on a line.

Again and again, the same thoughts kept running through his mind, increasing his sense of anxiety. He felt as if he was caught in a maze without an end, and round every unseen corner lurked monsters waiting to pounce.

He started to feel like something was watching them – something vast and malevolent – a presence all around them.

What she saw next changed things completely.

A tingling sixth sense made him look up. As he turned, he froze.

Their optimism lasted only a moment.

She thought they had escaped; at least she thought it was safe until she saw what waited for them at the top.

Panic welled up inside her as she felt the familiar shiver. She turned but there was no one there.

Every muscle in her body tensed. Something was about to go terribly wrong.

There was no time to ask questions – there was only time to survive.

He knew his life hung by a thread.

He staggered a little as he went on, and wondered what else would try to hinder him from reaching his goal.

For fatal seconds, they stared, unable to think or move. And, as they faltered, the jaws of the trap closed about them.

His heart shrivelled with fear when he looked down and saw how high up he was.

Fear slithered around her like a dark fog, bringing a damp chill that gradually crept over her, even though she was sweating with the effort of the climb.

It was as if time had stopped. She shuddered and went rigid, as if frozen to the spot.

Every movement was an effort, fighting to breathe, forcing himself to keep moving.

He slithered to a halt, and stood hands on hips, head bowed, his breath coming in painful gasps.

She was starting to lose all memory of how to move her aching limbs. Her heart pounded like a drum and panic was beginning to set in.

She felt battered and bruised, utterly exhausted. She had reached her limit. She couldn't go on. Her body was shutting down. Her muscles ached with the sickening pain. It was as if someone had sprinkled red-hot needles across her arms and legs.

Just staying on her feet was a monumental task of sheer willpower and determination.

Every nerve in his body screamed at him as the pain gripped his shoulder like a clenched fist.

Every step sent a shock wave of pain through his ankle.

A trickle of blood dripped down his forehead, and into his mouth. It was what he needed to jolt him out of his paralysis and kick-start his survival instincts. He had to move. And soon.

He slumped to the ground with his hands on his knees, gasping for each painful breath, and when he eventually managed to speak, his voice was a low, painful wheeze.

He knew that their epic struggle was coming to an end. They had nearly reached the top of the mountain. They were tantalisingly close, but their bodies were weakening with every step.

She moved her lips silently in prayer.

Drawing in a deep breath, she blew it out hard to stop herself howling and force herself to keep calm . . . keep moving.

He was starting to become delirious, muttering, rambling, groaning.

She stared unblinking above her, as if in a trance and frozen to the spot.

5

Forests

The forest was an endless labyrinth of towering trees – an unending green blanket steeped in shadow. As the forest closed in around them, their **unease grew. They knew that its dark recesses could conceal any number of dangers and ambushes.** Every few steps, they kept glancing nervously over their shoulders, probing the forest for any flicker of movement, **expecting to see something hideous in every shadow**.

As they wound their way through the forest, they stalked amongst the trees without the snap of a twig to betray them. However, the deeper into the forest they went, **the more uneasy Rob was becoming. At every sound, every shadow, he fingered his bow nervously. He couldn't shake off the strange sensation that he was being followed.**

The forest was usually teeming with life, but it had fallen strangely silent. Even though **her heart was thudding wildly in her chest, Kitty knew she had to keep moving.** When she heard a faint noise behind her, she risked a quick glance over her shoulder . . . no one there.

Then, suddenly, without any warning, the silence was shattered by the rattle of armour, the thundering of hooves, the distinctive whistle of an arrow. Kitty hurtled back towards the trees . . . the safety and cover of the shadows. Easing herself sideways, she kept the trunk between her and the approaching riders. **She moved her lips silently in prayer. They couldn't catch her now!** There was nothing she could do but stay dead still, press herself against the tree, and hope she wouldn't be seen.

SECTION 1 – SETTING

WORDS

Nouns	**Clearing**, track, path, trail
	Maze, labyrinth, corridor, passageway, gaps, recesses
	Trees, bushes, canopy, trunks, bark, branches, boughs, twigs, leaves, roots, undergrowth, bogs, swamps, mud
	Thorns, brambles, creepers, weeds, pine needles
	Owl, crows, rooks, hawk
	Wolf, hounds
	Horse, hooves, bridle, harness
	Soldier, armour, chain mail, hunters, outlaws
	Quiver, bow, bowstring, arrow, tip, arrowhead
	Footsteps, shouts, yells
	Hiss, whistle, twang, clink, clang, rattle
	Hoot, howl, snort
Similes/ Metaphors	***Unending green blanket**; like melting wax; like barbed wire; grasping limbs; like lots of sharp fingernails; like a cunningly laid tripwire; as if the forest was holding its breath; like a pistol shot*
Adjectives	**Dark**, gloomy
	Unseen, invisible
	Cold, chilly, icy
	Thick, dense, pathless, impenetrable, endless
	Tall, high, vast, towering
	Gnarled, twisted, interlocking
	Wild, ancient
	Sudden, occasional
	Strange, eerie, silent, faint, muffled
	Snapping, cracking, crackling, splintering, jangling, clinking, thundering
	Bare, bony, mossy, rotting, matted, peeling, dead, decayed
	Vicious, barbed, ankle-twisting, dangerous, treacherous
	Yew, oak, birch, willow

Verbs	
	Surrounded, stretched, dotted, wrapped, covered
	Twisted, turned
	Grew, narrowed, pressed, closed, blocked
	Littered, strangled, choked
	Sheltered, hid, concealed, camouflaged
	Tugged, grasped, grabbed, clasped, clutched, tripped
	Darkened, shrouded
	Ran, headed, plunged, wound, struggled through, doubled back, carried on
	Ducked, crashed through, leaped, vaulted
	Rose, burst, flew, descended, spiralled
	Looked, peered, saw, watched
	Heard, hissed, smacked, clattered, jangled, echoed
	Approached, thundered

PHRASES – NOUNS AND ADJECTIVES

- ★ Every so often
- ★ Within minutes
- ★ All at once
- ★ Without warning
- ★ *All the way through the forest*
- ★ In the distance
- ★ From somewhere ahead
- ★ In that part of the forest
- ★ In the clearing
- ★ Behind them
- ★ Ahead of him
- ★ Through the leaves
- ★ On either side of the track
- ★ Past their heads
- ★ *Ancient, pathless forest*
- ★ An endless labyrinth of trees
- ★ An unending, green blanket
- ★ Every towering tree, every trunk, every trail
- ★ *Vast gnarled oak tree*
- ★ Mossy oaks with trunks like melting wax
- ★ Birches with peeling, white bark
- ★ Knuckled roots
- ★ Splintered trunks

- *No easy paths*
- No straight lines – limited visibility
- Tight interlocking branches
- Impenetrable walls of thorns and brambles
- Dense undergrowth
- *Corridors between the tall yew trees*
- Dark recesses
- Hollow, darkened passageway
- Darkened space between the trees
- Clouds of steamy mist
- *Twisted boughs*
- Dead branches and hidden roots
- Patches of brambles, fallen trees, boggy strips
- Matted creepers
- Mat of creeping, dark green weed
- A thick layer of pine needles
- Roots, thorns and grasping limbs
- Treacherous, ankle-twisting path
- *Unseen owls*
- Hunting owls
- Hunting hawk
- Murder of crows
- *Strangely silent*
- Faint footsteps
- Sound of a snapping twig
- Crackling in the canopy above their heads
- Shouts of alarm
- *Howl of a wolf*
- Loud hoot
- Blast of a hunting horn
- Belling of the hounds
- Horse's snort
- Faint rattle of a bridle
- Jangling of a harness
- Thundering hooves
- A handful of shadowy figures on horseback
- A rattle of armour
- Sound of many hunters
- Occasional clink of his bow
- Distinctive whistle of an arrow
- Twang of a bowstring
- Flight of arrows
- Volley of fire arrows
- Hiss of an arrow

PHRASES – VERBS

* As he was about to return to camp . . .
* As if the forest was holding its breath
* Twisted and turned
* Dictated which way they could move
* Impossible to follow a straight course
* Had to find higher ground or climb a tree
* *Closed in on him*
* Pressed in closer to the trail
* Blocked the path
* Blocked any access
* Stretched across the forest floor
* Climbed almost horizontally out of the ground
* Seemed to get narrower with every step
* Covered the full width of the path
* Could not penetrate the ancient tangle
* Only visible to those who knew the forest
* *Headed towards . . .*
* Headed deeper into the forest
* Plunged into the wood
* Wound their way through the wood
* Struggled on, doubling back time and again
* Carried on until they came to a clearing
* *Dotted with vicious thorns*
* Wrapped in vines
* Made a natural ladder up into the canopy
* Choked with dead wood and leaves
* Littered with treacherous bogs
* Camouflaged by dead leaves and slippery lichen
* Threw up ankle-twisting, gnarled roots
* Ran through the semi-darkness like barbed wire
* *Tugged at her feet*
* Tried to trip her up
* Grabbed at them like lots of sharp fingernails
* Ducked under low branches
* Climbed over fallen trees
* Crashed through the vines
* *Steeped in shadow*
* Formed a gloomy vault
* Surrounded by blackness on all sides
* Peered into the black spaces between the trees
* Darkened the already gloomy evening
* Loomed out of the shadows

- ☆ Shrouded in mist
- ☆ *Could conceal any number of dangers*
- ☆ Imagined the trees had grown eyes
- ☆ *Caught a movement on the edge of his vision*
- ☆ Rose from the woodland floor
- ☆ Flew above them like a white shadow
- ☆ Filled the night sky
- ☆ Circled above the branches
- ☆ Burst from the trees
- ☆ Rose in a flurry
- ☆ Spiralled down towards the trees
- ☆ *Usually teeming with life*
- ☆ Fell quiet
- ☆ Waiting to exhale when the danger had passed
- ☆ *Muffled their footsteps*
- ☆ Heard a faint noise
- ☆ Heard the sound of voices
- ☆ *Cracked out like a pistol shot*
- ☆ Drowned by the flapping of hundreds of wings
- ☆ Echoed through the forest
- ☆ *Approached them from behind*
- ☆ Approached slowly through the forest
- ☆ Vaulted over the rise and into view
- ☆ Came thundering out of the mist
- ☆ *Swept overhead*
- ☆ Hissed into the camp from unseen attackers
- ☆ Smacked into the trunk of a tree
- ☆ Clattered into the trees
- ☆ *Shot through the dark*
- ☆ Sliced through the sky in a blazing arc
- ☆ Left a trail of fiery light

SENTENCES

The forest was an endless labyrinth of trees – an unending green blanket. Every towering tree, every trunk, every trail looked like the one before.

The trees grew densely in that part of the forest – mossy oaks with trunks like melting candles, birches with peeling white bark.

The trunks were wrapped in vines that grew in all directions, making a natural ladder up into the canopy.

The forest closed around them – huge, ancient oaks with knuckled roots and splintered trunks spreading into an arched ceiling.

The trail twisted and turned. As they headed deeper into the forest, the trees seemed to get thicker and press in closer to narrow the trail even further.

The bushes dictated which direction they could move. It was not easy as there were no straight lines and visibility was limited unless they found higher ground or climbed a tree.

There were no easy paths. They struggled on, doubling back time and again as the going grew too difficult.

It was an old, pathless forest, and it was impossible to follow a straight course. Patches of brambles, fallen trees, strips of bog and dense undergrowth blocked the path.

The path to their camp was completely overgrown, but still visible to those who knew the forest – marked from its surroundings by a mat of creeping, dark green weed.

They carried on until they came to a small clearing where the path seemed to end.

The corridors between the tall yew trees were steeped in shadow.

The shadows deepened, stretching across the forest floor.

The track seemed to get narrower with every step until the wood swallowed them whole; the branches darkened the already gloomy evening.

There was a growing unease among them as they wound their way through the wood, knowing that its dark recesses could conceal any number of dangers and ambushes.

The tight interlocking branches formed a gloomy vault. It felt like she was going down a hollow, darkened passageway and it was easy to imagine someone or something watching her from the darkened spaces between the trees.

Even the moonlight could not penetrate the ancient tangle of roots, thorns and grasping limbs, but every so often the trunk of a tree would loom out of the shadows.

It was a treacherous, ankle-twisting path. He had to watch his footing – there were dead branches and hidden roots everywhere, camouflaged by rotting leaves and slippery lichen.

They crashed through vines dotted with vicious thorns that ran through the gloom like barbed wire and grabbed at them like lots of sharp fingernails.

The ground was boggy and choked with dead wood and leaves. Progress was slow as they kept having to duck under low branches and climb over fallen trees.

A vast gnarled oak tree climbed almost horizontally out of the ground; its twisted boughs covered the full width of the path and blocked any access.

The dense undergrowth tugged at her feet, trying to trip her, throwing up ankle-twisting, gnarled roots and impenetrable walls of thorns and brambles.

Something tripped him and he sprawled headlong – a vine stretched across the path like a cunningly laid tripwire.

The forest was utterly silent. It was as if it was holding its breath, waiting to exhale when the danger had passed.

The forest was usually teeming with life, but it was strangely silent.

Not a thing stirred in the trees. The only sounds were his own faint footsteps and the occasional clink of his bow against his belt.

The sound of a snapping twig cracked out like a pistol shot.

The rooks fell quiet. Then rose in a flurry, circled once and spiralled down towards the trees.

The howl of a wolf in the distance was swiftly drowned out by the flapping of hundreds of wings.

A murder of crows rose from the trees; their caw, caw, caw filled the night sky as they circled above the branches.

A hunting owl burst from the tree with a loud hoot and flew above them like a white shadow.

High above them, a hunting hawk circled.

A thick layer of pine needles muffled their footfalls.

They had not walked far when he began to hear the sound of voices coming from somewhere ahead.

The sound of creaking, snapping and breaking branches filled the air.

He had just entered the forest when he heard the haunting blast of a hunting horn.

As he was about to return to the camp, he heard a faint noise: a horse's snort, the faint rattling of a bridle and, then, the distinctive whistle of an arrow.

He heard it again, the belling of the hounds, the thundering of hooves approaching them from behind. Then, a shout, the rattle of armour – the sound of many men hunting. A handful of shadowy figures on horseback suddenly vaulted over the rise and into view.

The sound was coming from behind him. The sound of hooves, the jangling of harness, a number of horses approaching slowly through the forest.

There was a twang of bowstrings as arrows let fly, and suddenly soldiers came thundering out of the mist.

A flight of arrows whispered through the dark. Another volley of arrows swept overhead and clattered against the trees. The archers were nowhere to be seen. More arrows hissed into the camp from the unseen attackers.

Shouts of alarm echoed through the forest as a volley of fire arrows sliced through the sky in a blazing arc towards them, leaving a trail of fiery light on the ground.

The first bolt shot through the dark, past their heads, smacking into the trunk of a tree just metres away. Then another and another.

SECTION 2 – INTERACTION

WORDS	

Nouns	**Bushes**, undergrowth, trees, saplings, branches, twigs, roots, logs, vines, brambles, thorns, grass
	Hill, slope, bank, ground
	Track, trail, path
	Shelter, cover, safety, hiding place, camp
	Light, shadows, gloom
	Rider, horse, hooves, bridle, stirrups, reins
	Weapon, sword, sheath, bow, arrow, quiver, staff, net
	Sound, rattle, jangle
	Movement, pursuers
Similes/ Metaphors	*As delicate as a wild creature; like fugitives; petrified as a statue; wooden claws of a branch*
Adjectives	**Ancient**, narrow
	Dim, faint
	Dense, impenetrable
	Patchy, uneven, random
	Flattened, squashed, trampled
	Gnarled, rugged, crooked, twisted
Verbs	**Moved**, walked, stalked, looped, circled
	Cleared, slashed, sliced
	Waited, stopped, halted, stood
	Ducked, dived, flung, threw
	Sat, crouched, huddled, pressed, flattened, burrowed
	Eased, inched, edged, crawled

Rushed, galloped, ran, raced, darted, dashed, sprinted, bolted, hurtled, outran, outpaced

Slipped, skidded, slid, stumbled, blundered, scrambled

Fell, dropped, crashed, catapulted

Groped, flung out

Grasped, clutched, tangled, caught, whipped, smacked, tripped

Leapt up, lunged, reached, grabbed, seized, pulled, pushed off, let go, released

Climbed, shimmied, hopped, swung

Rose, raised, looked, glanced, peeked, peered, flickered, probed, searched, scoured, strained, watched

Heard, hissed, rattled

Pulled, gripped, fitted, notched, nocked, drew, aimed, fired

PHRASES – NOUNS AND ADJECTIVES

* One moment . . . the next . . .
* *From her hiding place*
* In the bushes to his left
* Somewhere nearby
* Top of the hill
* Behind him
* Behind the tree
* Towards the trees
* *In the shadows*
* Safety and cover of the shadows
* Dim light
* *Narrow track*
* Ancient yew tree
* Gnarled branches
* Wooden claws of a branch
* Patchy, flattened grass
* *Faint sound*
* Sound of a snapping twig
* Faint rattle of a bridle
* Approaching riders
* *Out of range*
* Only paces from him
* *On the tips of his toes*
* Motionless and alert

- *Unable to move, rigid with fear*
- Petrified as a statue
- *Flailing hand*
- As delicately as a wild creature
- Like fugitives
- Head down, legs a blur of movement

PHRASES – VERBS

- As the trail became more difficult to follow . . .
- Until he made the shelter of the trees . . .
- *As they hunted for him . . .*
- As he heard the sound of hooves behind him . . .
- As he heard an arrow hissing through the air . . .
- *When he tried to quicken his pace . . .*
- One minute, he was walking along the track, the next . . .
- *Worked her way through the forest*
- Stalked amongst the trees
- Walked backwards in a circle
- Looped round the camp towards the trees
- Landed on the trail behind them
- *Cleared a way forward*
- Slashed at the dense undergrowth
- Sliced through the grasping vines that dangled in front of him
- Used his staff to force a path through it
- *Listened to the sound from . . .*
- Strained for any sound
- Heard something
- Heard the sounds of shifting armour
- Cracked out like a pistol shot
- Warned him that at least one of his pursuers stood close by
- *Strained to see*
- Peered into the shadows
- Looked all about him
- Looked from side to side and over her shoulders
- Probed the forest for a flicker of movement
- Darted from side to side,
- Checked for any movement
- Risked a quick glance over his shoulder
- *Indicated to the others that they should . . .*
- Signalled with his hands
- Raised his hand to signal someone was coming
- *Lingered in the shadows*

- ★ Stopped when she reached the narrow track
- ★ Stopped dead in his tracks
- ★ Hadn't moved a muscle for five minutes
- ★ Waited, watched . . . still did not move
- ★ Nothing she could do but sit dead still
- ★ Counted to ten before daring to look
- ★ *Pressed herself against the tree*
- ★ Ducked down low
- ★ Ducked behind a tree
- ★ Dived under a bush
- ★ Flung himself down behind a tree
- ★ Threw herself down on the top of the hill
- ★ *Crouched behind the . . .*
- ★ Flattened herself against the ground
- ★ Pressed himself closer to the ground
- ★ Burrowed deeper into his thorny hiding place
- ★ *Raised her head cautiously*
- ★ Peered through the branches
- ★ Rose to take another look
- ★ Peered out and squinted into the darkness
- ★ Watched from underneath the bush
- ★ Looked down without being spotted
- ★ *Could not make out anything*
- ★ Could not make out the features of their faces
- ★ *Eased herself sideways*
- ★ Kept low and in the shadows
- ★ Kept the trunk between her and the approaching rider
- ★ *Crawled out of the forest as fast as she dared*
- ★ Crawled backwards out of range
- ★ Carefully placed her hands and feet on the patches of long grass
- ★ Prayed that the grass would spring back into position behind her
- ★ *Dashed to the other side of the trail, out of sight*
- ★ Scrambled up the bank
- ★ Darted forward
- ★ Hurtled back towards the trees
- ★ Darted and dodged through the trees
- ★ Changed direction quickly
- ★ Raced towards the undergrowth
- ★ Ran blindly, taking no notice of distance or direction
- ★ Ran like a wild creature
- ★ Tried to outpace his pursuers
- ★ Kept on running, arms pumping, her lungs burning
- ★ Never once did she turn and look back
- ★ *Lost his footing many times*

- ⭑ Couldn't tell where he was going
- ⭑ Stumbled blindly through the undergrowth
- ⭑ Crashed to the ground
- ⭑ Groped for something to stop her falling
- ⭑ Flung her hand out in front of her
- ⭑ Blundered and slipped
- ⭑ Fought his way through the undergrowth
- ⭑ Slid down through the undergrowth
- ⭑ *Fell over roots and branches*
- ⭑ Crashed into trees and tangled his legs in brambles
- ⭑ Tangled in a thick tree root and fell headlong
- ⭑ Stumbled into the wooden claws of a branch
- ⭑ Tripped by saplings and fallen logs looming out of nowhere
- ⭑ Whipped by unseen, sharp branches
- ⭑ Clutched at his arms as he pounded past
- ⭑ Whizzed by him
- ⭑ Smacked at his face when he couldn't duck fast enough
- ⭑ *Catapulted into the air by a large net*
- ⭑ Covered by leaves and branches and attached to a tree
- ⭑ *Leapt up and threw himself at a lower branch of the tree*
- ⭑ Grasped the branch and scrambled upwards
- ⭑ Swung her legs, wrapping them around the branch
- ⭑ Pulled herself on to the branch
- ⭑ Reached from branch to branch
- ⭑ Found a fork in the branches where she could sit
- ⭑ Climbed along the branch
- ⭑ Hopped onto the next tree
- ⭑ Shimmied out on the branch and reached for the next one
- ⭑ Swung herself off the branch
- ⭑ Used his legs to push off from the tree
- ⭑ Let go of the vine and seized another mid-air
- ⭑ Dropped to the ground
- ⭑ *Everyone moved, rushing for weapons, running for their horses*
- ⭑ Galloped past
- ⭑ Stood upright in her stirrups
- ⭑ *Leaped out, drawing her bow*
- ⭑ Drew an arrow from his quiver
- ⭑ Gripped the bow in her left hand
- ⭑ Nocked his bow
- ⭑ Notched an arrow, aimed and fired
- ⭑ *Pulled his sword from its sheath*
- ⭑ Drew her sword and led the way down the path

SENTENCES

Pulling his sword from its sheath, he started slashing at the dense undergrowth to clear a way forward.

The foliage thickened and, as the trail became more difficult to follow, he used his staff to force a path through it.

He listened to the faint sound from behind him and indicated to the others that they should move to either side of the trail, out of sight.

When he raised his hand to signal something was coming, the others immediately ducked down low.

Scrambling up the bank, she flattened herself against the ground.

He crouched behind the tree, motionless, his ears straining for any sound, his eyes peering into the shadows.

Frantically, looking from side to side and over her shoulders, she ducked behind a tree.

He flung himself down behind a tree and nocked his bow.

Hearing the sounds of shifting armour, he trembled and burrowed deeper into his thorny hiding place, ignoring the pain as the needle-sharp leaves pierced his skin.

Diving under a bush, she pressed herself flat against the ground and waited. She counted to ten before daring to look. They hadn't seen her, yet! If she had any chance of escape, she had to move now.

The sound of a snapping twig cracked out like a pistol shot, warning him that at least of one his pursuers stood only paces from him. He strained to see him but could make out nothing, not so much as a moving shadow in the gloom. He pressed himself closer to the ground.

From her hiding place, she could not make out the features of their faces, so she couldn't be sure it was them, but a sixth sense warned her that it was, that they had picked up her trail. She was unable to move, rigid with fear.

There was nothing she could do but sit dead still and press herself against the tree and hope she wouldn't be seen.

He watched from underneath the bush as they hunted for him.

She was crouched behind the ancient yew tree. She hadn't moved a muscle for five minutes. She waited, watched . . . still did not move.

Motionless and alert, they lingered in the shadows, ready to move quickly. They watched and waited. Then, slowly, Tom peered out and squinted into the darkness. His eyes darted left and right, probing the forest for a flicker of movement.

On the tips of his toes, he rose to take another look.

Raising her head cautiously, she peered through the branches.

He walked backwards in a circle, looking all about him.

He crawled backwards, out of range.

She crawled out of the forest and into the meadow as fast as she dared. Very carefully, she placed her hands and feet on the patches of long grass, praying that it would spring back into position behind her and conceal her movements.

She stopped when she reached the narrow track. She had heard something . . . the snap of a twig, the faint rattle of a bridle. She hurtled back towards the trees . . . the safety and cover of the shadows. Easing herself sideways, she kept the trunk between her and the approaching rider.

He stopped dead in his tracks as he heard the sound of hooves behind him. Quickly, he changed direction, raced towards the undergrowth and ducked behind a tree.

Darting forward, Kitty kept low and threw herself down on the top of the hill behind the tree so that she could look down without being spotted.

She ran blindly, taking no notice of distance or direction. Every sense became sharpened and she moved as delicately as a wild creature, avoiding twigs and loose stones.

Never once did she turn and look back . . . just kept on running, arms pumping, her lungs burning.

He darted and dodged through the trees. Blundering and slipping, he fought his way through the undergrowth grasping at his ankles.

Keeping low, and in the shadows, she ran back, looping round the camp towards the trees.

He ran on, falling over roots and branches, crashing into trees and tangling his legs in brambles. He risked a quick glance over his shoulder as he heard an arrow hissing through the air somewhere nearby.

He ran like a wild creature, trying to outpace his pursuers, until he made the shelter of the thick trees.

Clenching his fists, he ran. The trees whizzed by him, their gnarled branches clutching at his arms as he pounded past.

He lost his footing so many times, he gave up and slid down through the undergrowth, branches smacking at his face when he couldn't duck fast enough.

She turned and fled, but fell over a tree root, stumbling onto her face, stunned as her head made sharp contact with the ground.

She stumbled and flung her hand out in front of her, groping for something to stop her falling.

The ground was uneven, so when he tried to quicken his pace, he stumbled, crashing to the ground.

One moment he was stumbling blindly through the undergrowth, the next, his feet tangled in a thick tree root and he fell headlong.

The darkness was so complete he couldn't tell where he was going. He stumbled into the wooden claws of a trunk, was whipped by unseen, sharp branches and tripped by saplings and fallen logs looming out of nowhere.

One minute he was walking along the track, and the next he was catapulted into the air by a large net. It had been covered by leaves and branches and attached to a tree.

He leapt up and threw himself at a lower branch of the tree, grasped the branch and scrambled upwards.

Swinging her legs, wrapping them around the branch, she pulled herself on to it, then reached from branch to branch until she found a fork in the branches where she could sit and look out.

He climbed along the branch, and hopped onto the next tree.

He shimmied out on the branch and reached for the next one.

There was a cracking sound, and he swayed on the branch. He was too far from the trunk and the branch beneath his feet was splintering and about to give way.

The branch dipped dangerously low, threatening to snap and send him spiralling to the ground.

She swung herself off the branch and dropped to the ground.

Using his legs, Tom pushed off from the tree, let go of the vine and seized another mid-air.

Suddenly, everyone was moving, reaching for weapons, running to their horses.

A path branched off to the right; its patchy grass showed signs of being recently trampled. She drew her sword and led the way, eyes darting from side to side, checking for any movement.

Working her way through the forest, she stalked amongst the trees without the snap of a twig to betray her. When she neared their position, she leaped out, drawing her bow, landing on the trail behind them.

He drew an arrow from his quiver, notched it, aimed and fired.

She galloped past, standing upright in her stirrups, her reins dangling loose, a bow gripped in her left hand.

SECTION 3 – REACTION

WORDS

Nouns

Instant, moment, split-second

Presence, shadows

Instinct, feeling, thoughts, senses, sensation

Adrenalin, nerves, muscles, sweat

Panic, urgency

Shock, fear, fright, dread, terror

Brain, heart, pulse, temples, chest, breath, cheeks

Body, stomach, shoulder, spine, neck, arm, hand, face, eyes

Voice, whisper, sob, shout, scream, howl, shriek

Similes/ Metaphors

Like an electric shock; a shivering wave of terror

Adjectives

Raw, blind, sheer, tight

Sixth, tingling, prickling

Low, slow, halting

Chilly, icy, steely

Alert, wide, staring, urgent

Pounding, thudding, hammering

Desperate, frantic, rasping, jagged, halting

Menacing, hideous

Verbs

Expected, discovered, anticipated, warned, knew, realised, remembered, recalled

Squashed, repressed, suppressed

Felt, sensed, imagined

Pounded, thudded, hammered, charged, surged

Held, drew, sucked, gasped, steadied, blew out

Gritted, gnashed, clenched

Looked, flickered, darted, swept, strained

Spoke, dropped, lowered, whispered

Fingered, clutched, gripped

PHRASES – NOUNS AND ADJECTIVES

- In that one instant
- But the next moment
- From a little way off
- Away from the camp, deeper into the woods
- *Raw instinct*
- Blind instinct
- Sheer panic
- Utterly alert
- Every nerve in his body
- Every muscle in her body
- Beads of sweat
- Tingling sixth sense
- Tight knot in her stomach
- Surge of adrenalin
- Like an electric shock
- *Wide and staring*
- Urgent and twisted with terror
- *Horse's snort, rattle of a bridle*
- Distinctive whistle of an arrow
- Clang of metal on metal

PHRASES – VERBS

- As he crept through the forest . . .
- All her senses were on high alert
- Even though his heart was pounding . . .
- If she had any chance of escape . . .
- Realised he had run in the wrong direction
- Registered a menacing presence lurking in the shadows
- *Tried to remember the way back to the camp*
- Could not afford to get lost in the wood
- *Knew he had to remain calm*
- Repressed the rising tide of panic
- Forced herself to . . .
- Tried to anticipate their next move
- Tried to discover where the archer was hiding
- *Had to move now*
- Could not relay the message to her legs in time
- *Expected to see something hideous in every shadow*
- Afraid something or someone was following her
- Warned her that she was walking into trouble

- *Felt a chill, steely fist squeeze her heart*
- Reeling with fright
- Clenched and thudded in her chest
- Sent a shivering wave of terror down his spine
- Pounded in her temples
- Charged down his spine like an electric shock
- Strained to breaking point
- Tensed and ready to run
- *Blew out her cheeks*
- Drew a rasping, jagged breath
- Held their breath
- Gasped for breath
- Could hardly breathe
- Clenched his jaw
- Gnashed his teeth together
- Terrified to make a noise
- *Darted to and fro*
- Darted wildly from side to side
- Flickered nervously left and right
- Swept the scene in front of her
- Strained to pierce the darkness
- Made her look up
- Looked furtively over her shoulder
- Risked a glance over his shoulder
- Glanced fearfully around
- Looked at one another
- Exchanged a nervous glance
- *Dropped to an urgent whisper*
- Spoke in a low, halting voice
- No one said a word
- Dared not swallow
- Feared they would hear her
- Steadied himself, holding his breath
- *Strained for the sound of the approaching horses*
- Heard a faint noise
- *Slithered to a halt*
- Froze her to the spot
- Turned her head, and froze
- Fingered his bow nervously

SENTENCES

As he crept through the forest, beads of sweat broke out across his forehead. He fingered his bow nervously, his hand stiff.

Her heart clenched and thudded in her chest. She had to force herself to struggle to her feet. If she had any chance of escape, she had to move now.

Her brain registered a menacing presence lurking in the shadows, but she was unable to relay the message to her legs in time.

Reeling with fright, he realised that he had run in the wrong direction – away from the camp, deeper into the woods.

A shiver charged down his spine like an electric shock.

A tight knot in her stomach warned Gail that she was walking into trouble, but she knew she had to warn them at all costs.

Even though his heart was pounding, he knew he had to remain calm and repress the rising tide of panic. He could not afford to get lost in the wood.

Raw instinct took control as a surge of adrenalin shot through her. Every muscle in her body was tensed and ready to run.

A tingling sixth sense made her look up. As she turned her head, she froze. A cowled figure had stepped out from behind a bush. He was holding something in his hands. Her stomach lurched as she realised that it was a crossbow . . . nocked . . . the arrow aimed directly at her.

All her senses were on high alert as she strained for the sound of the approaching riders.

He felt as if there were eyes everywhere, following his every move.

Her eyes darted to and fro, sweeping the scene in front of her, trying to discover where the archer was hiding.

She looked furtively over her shoulder, as if she was afraid something or someone was following her.

Their eyes flickered quickly upwards.

Her eyes swept over the scene in front of her as she tried to anticipate their next move.

He risked a quick glance over his shoulder.

She glanced fearfully around, expecting to see something hideous in every shadow.

Blowing out her cheeks, she drew a rasping, jagged breath.

They all held their breath. From a little way off, they heard a faint noise: a horse's snort, the faint rattling of a bridle and then the distinctive whistle of an arrow.

His voice dropped to an urgent whisper.

They looked at one another, but no one said a word.

She dared not swallow for fear they would hear her.

She steadied herself, holding her breath.

Clenching his jaw, he gnashed his teeth together, too terrified to make a noise.

He spoke in a low, halting voice, constantly looking from side to side.

6
Caves

Cautiously, they edged their way through the gap and emerged in an enormous cave the size of a cathedral. Along the left-hand wall, strange letters and geometric shapes had been carved and scraped into the surface.

They moved along the wall, leaning closer to get a better look at the drawings. All of a sudden, Kitty stopped dead in her tracks. She had noticed a movement out of the corner of her eye. Ahead of them, rays of light, like ghostly fingers, had suddenly filtered through from a gap somewhere high above their heads. Where the light fell on the wall, it had lit up a dragon that had been painted over the entrance to the next cave, its vast wings stretching across the arch. **For some reason, the painting sent a chill shivering down Kitty's spine, as if someone was pushing ice-cold needles into the back of her neck.**

SECTION 1 – SETTING

WORDS

Nouns	**Mouth**, hole, gap, entrance, side, edge, centre
	Inside, interior, pit, bowels
	Cavern, chamber, passage, gallery, columns, pillars, arches, crypt, vault, tomb, walls, roof, floor, ground
	Water, stream, pool, lake
	Stalagmites, stalactites, icicles, crystals
	Carvings, etchings, pictures, scenes, signs, symbols, paint, chalk
	Horses, deer, stags, unicorns, dragons, phoenix, griffins, eagle, bull, bison, boar, bear, bird-headed man

Statue, warrior, sculpture, effigy, king, sword

Skeletons, bones, skull

Roots, vines, moss, lichen

Sound, voice, hiss, shriek, laughter, echo

Light, rays, torch, beam, brazier

Darkness, shadows

Smell, stench, water, damp, mould, peat, chalk, flint, sulphur, decay

Similes/ Metaphors	*Like a silent, screaming mouth; like a cathedral; like a secret, ancient vault; like enormous diamonds; like giant crystal spikes; like a crystal chandelier; like glistening spears of light; like a forest of stalagmites; as cold as a crypt; as dark as night; like ghostly fingers; like marble; like a bubbling rock soup; like manacles around her wrists; like being sucked down into the depths of the earth*
Adjectives	**Huge**, life-sized, giant, enormous, monumental
	Low, high, deep
	Secret, ancient
	Dark, black, inky, gloomy, dim, shadowy, ghostly, spectral
	Eerie, sinister, empty, lifeless, powerful, menacing
	Flickering, dancing
	Cold, icy, freezing, damp, clammy
	Colourful, vivid, rich, life-like, detailed, realistic
	White, blue, red, gold, green, brown
	Luminous, phosphorescent
	Shimmering, glistening, glowing, jewelled, ornate, gilded
	Interlocking, linking, mathematical, geometrical
	Putrid, sickly, stale, sulphurous
	Rough, jagged, sharp, needle-sharp
	Hissing, sucking, snickering
Verbs	**Stretched**, opened, branched, divided, split, radiated
	Rose, hung, dangled, swooped, suspended, cascaded
	Sculpted, carved, etched, chiselled, engraved, chalked
	Daubed, flecked, speckled

Covered, littered

Lit, crept, cast, illuminated, pierced, reflected, flooded

Revealed, glimpsed, disappeared, vanished

Heard, floated, came from, surrounded by, filled

Boomed, crackled, crunched, dripped, echoed

Bubbled, trickled, gushed

Wafted, carried, drifted, brought

Rocked, cracked, thrashed, lashed, wrapped

Startled, spooked, alarmed

Tensed, braced, stiffened

PHRASES – NOUNS AND ADJECTIVES

* For a brief second
* *In one of the caves*
* At the entrance to the cave
* In the centre of the cave
* Deep in the bowels of the cave
* Beneath his feet
* Above his head
* Somewhere in the distance
* *Behind thick, tangled vines*
* In the face of the sheer, deadly slopes
* *Mouth of a low cave*
* Entrance to an enormous cave
* A ghostly black hole – a silent screaming mouth
* *An enormous cavern, the size of a cathedral*
* Gallery of columns
* Monumental arches
* Like a secret, ancient vault
* A hole in the rock the size of a small door
* *Huge, shimmering stalactites like enormous diamonds*
* Stalagmites like giant crystal spikes
* Glittering gallery of white crystals
* Like glistening spears of light
* Like a forest of stalagmites
* *Deep carvings*
* Strange letters from an ancient language
* Pictures of leaping white stags
* Scenes from a wild boar hunt

- Walls completely covered by paintings of four, enormous, black bulls
- Life-like hunting scenes
- Terrifying, bird-headed man
- Strange, interlocking, geometric symbols and signs
- Niches in the walls where lamps . . .
- Clammy, cold, icy to the touch
- As cold as a crypt and dark as night
- *Long buried and forgotten*
- *Not one ray of light*
- Nothing but impenetrable dark
- Rays of dim light like ghostly fingers
- *Eerie growl*
- Clouds of shrieking bats
- Dying echo in the freezing passage
- Humming sound
- Dripping water
- Eerie noise in the sinister stillness of the cave
- Sinister sucking, snickering sound
- Deep voice
- Sound of beating wings
- *Putrid, sickly stench*
- Waft of stale air
- Cobwebs and mould
- Smell of stagnant water and damp decay
- Smell of peat, chalk, flint and sulphur
- *Shimmering lake*
- Needle-sharp tipped vines
- Bones like rotten wood
- Hollow skull
- *Stone tomb*
- Figure of an enormous warrior
- Life-sized effigy of a king
- Jewelled sword

PHRASES – VERBS

- Carved out of the rocky wall
- Reached out into the shadows
- Stretched away in every direction
- Extended into the dark caves beyond
- Wound between . . .
- Branched off to the right
- *As they walked further into the cavern . . .*

* Found himself in . . .
* Opened out into . . .
* Rose high above their heads
* Suspended from the roof
* Hung like a crystal chandelier above his head
* Plunged from the roof
* Covered the floor
* Littered the floor
* Merged together to form solid, shimmering pillars
* Leaked in through the rocks
* Glistened with damp
* Shone like marble
* Bubbled through the middle of the cave
* Trickled under the cave wall
* Formed a pool of deep, glowing blue water
* *As his eyes got used to the dark . . .*
* Where light flooded into the cave . . .
* Caught a glimpse of . . .
* Disappeared out of sight
* Peered into the inky blackness
* *Reflected the light from his torch*
* Pierced the shadows around her
* Rose from the gloom
* Crept across the floor and walls
* Glowed with a phosphorescent light
* *Held the candle before her like a weapon*
* Swung it from side to side
* *Did little to push back the darkness*
* Saw a flickering light
* Filtered through from above
* Cast spectral shadows on the walls
* Cast dancing shadows across their path
* Noticed a shadow that seemed darker than the others
* *Heard a whisper of sound*
* Heard whispering laughter
* Floated towards her
* Seemed to be coming from inside the walls
* Came from the distance
* Surrounded by the echoes of . . .
* Boomed out of one of the tunnels
* Seemed treacherously loud
* Hissed through the darkness
* Filled with the sound of . . .
* Swooped from the ceiling

- *Covered in pictures of . . .*
- Etched into the stone walls
- Carved into the rock
- Daubed with swirling red and blue paint
- *Wafted against his face*
- Drifted through the air
- Brought a smell of . . .
- Like being sucked down into the depths of the earth
- *Rose from the bottom of the pit*
- Bubbled like soup
- Sent columns of sulphurous stench
- Gushed out into the fiery river of boiling lava
- *Rocked and cracked*
- Vines forced their way through the gaps
- Thrashed at the air
- Crept closer to her
- Wrapped around her ankle
- Lashed out to lock like manacles around her wrists
- *Felt a presence . . . cold, powerful, menacing*
- Edged further into the cave
- Startled by . . .
- Stood stiff, staring ahead with empty, lifeless eyes
- Stumbled over one of the many skeletons
- Littered the floor
- Cracked and shattered the bones

SENTENCES

Hidden behind thick, tangled vines was the mouth of a low cave that had been carved out of the rocky wall.

The cave was a black hole – a silent, screaming mouth in the face of the deadly slopes.

He found himself in a huge, circular cavern.

An enormous cavern, the size of a cathedral, stretched out into the shadows.

A gallery of columns stretched away in every direction around them; monumental arches rose high above their heads. It was like a secret, ancient vault long buried and forgotten.

The cavern was like a forest of stalagmites, narrow paths winding between them, stretching into the dark caves beyond.

Hanging from the roof, like enormous diamonds, were huge, shimmering stalactites. Stalagmites like giant, crystal spikes covered the floor.

The tunnel suddenly opened out into a glittering gallery of white crystals.

Icicles plunged from the roof to hang like a crystal chandelier above his head, reflecting the light from his torch back like glistening spears of light to pierce the shadows around him.

In one of the caves, the stalactites and stalagmites had merged together to form giant, solid, shimmering pillars.

Where water had leaked in through the rocks, the walls and floor glistened like marble.

They found deep carvings etched into the stone walls – strange letters from an ancient language, and pictures of leaping white stags, scenes from a wild boar hunt, and in one corner, what looked like a phoenix spreading its wings across the wall.

At the entrance to the cave, the walls were daubed with swirling red and blue paint. As they walked further into the cavern, they came across strange mathematical symbols and signs that had been chalked and scraped into the surface.

Moss that glowed with a phosphorescent light crept across the floor and the walls.

The cave was as cold as a crypt and dark as night. Not one ray of light. Nothing but impenetrable dark.

As his eyes grew used to the dark, he made out two amber, reptilian eyes staring back at him from the shadows.

She held the candle before her like a weapon, swinging it from side to side. But it did little to push back the darkness and its flame cast spectral shadows on the walls.

For a brief second, he thought he saw the flickering of a flame deep in the bowels of the cave.

Rays of dim light, like ghostly fingers, filtered through from a gap somewhere high above.

By the entrance, a metal brazier lit the way, casting dancing shadows across their path. To his right, he noticed a shadow that seemed darker than the others, creeping across the wall.

Where light flooded through an opening in the top of the cave, it created a cascading, shimmering waterfall of light on one of the walls.

From somewhere in the gloom, she heard whispering laughter floating towards her. It seemed to be coming from inside the walls.

The echo of her voice rebounded between the enormous stalactites.

The sound of dripping water from ahead of him made an eerie noise in the sinister stillness of the cave.

The sinister, sucking, snickering sound seemed to come from a distance, yet the echo surrounded him.

A deep voice boomed out of one of the tunnels stretching away from the cave.

Every step seemed treacherously loud in the cave.

An eerie growl stopped him dead in his tracks.

Something hissed through the darkness.

The air was filled with the sound of beating wings as clouds of shrieking bats swooped from the ceiling.

A cold, clammy air wafted against his face, bringing with it a smell of stagnant water and damp decay.

It felt like he was being sucked down into the depths of the earth as the smell of peat, chalk, flint and sulphur drifted through the air.

A stream bubbled through the middle of the cave and then trickled under the cave wall, where it formed a pool of deep, glowing blue water.

At the centre of the cave was a shimmering, silver lake.

Hot air rose from the bottom of the pit in the centre of the cavern, which bubbled like soup, sending columns of a sulphurous stench to gush out into a fiery river of boiling lava.

As the stones started to rock and crack, needle-sharp vines forced their way into the gaps, thrashing at the air, creeping closer to her, until they were near enough to wrap around her legs and lock like handcuffs around her ankles.

As she entered one of the smaller caves set into the side, she felt a presence . . . cold, powerful, menacing. She edged further in, and was startled by the figure of an enormous warrior, clad in mail, visored helmet and armed with a sword. It stood stiff, staring ahead with empty, lifeless eyes.

He stumbled over one of the many skeletons that littered the floor, the bones cracking and shattering like rotten wood beneath his feet.

In the centre of the cave was a stone tomb. Lying along the top was a life-sized sculpture of a warrior, his jewelled sword clenched in his hand by his side.

SECTION 2 – INTERACTION

WORDS	
Nouns	**Cavern**, chamber, opening, hole, archway, niches, pillars
	Passage, path, slope, wall, ground, floor, ledge, chasm, abyss, tomb

Rocks, stones, gravel, dirt, dust

Cover, shelter, safety

Lake, pool, river, stream

Darkness, gloom, light, lamp, torch, beam, glare

Air, wind, blast

Bats, skulls, skeleton, serpents, hooves, vines

Cudgel, spear, dagger, blade, sword, hilt, sheath, bow, arrow

Body, back, arms, shoulders, elbows, hands, wrists, fingers, knuckles, legs, knees, feet, footholds

Bones, muscles, sinew

Effort, strain

Similes/ Metaphors	***Quiet as a grave***; *stalactites like spears; like a black plume of smoke; a hair's breadth*
Adjectives	**Huge**, vast, echoing
	Narrow, steep, precipitous
	Rocky, jagged, rough-hewn
	Damp, slippery, loose, dangerous, treacherous
	Fiery, burning, boiling, raging
	Wary, cautious, terrified
Verbs	**Ventured**, crossed, descended
	Entered, emerged, reached, came to, arrived at
	Squeezed, eased
	Raised, motioned, indicated
	Felt, groped, jerked, flapped
	Stopped, halted, froze
	Dropped, ducked, dived
	Crouched, hugged, pressed, flattened
	Rolled, flipped, crawled, scuttled
	Shuffled, edged, inched
	Moved, stepped, walked
	Quickened, rushed, darted, ran, raced, sprinted, surged, hurtled

Sprang, leapt, launched

Climbed, scrambled, clambered, hauled

Hung, dangled

Struggled, clawed, flailed

Slipped, slid, skidded, stumbled

Fell, toppled, plunged, plummeted

Landed, crashed

Knocked, threw, sent, slammed, seized

Glimpsed, stared, peered, glanced

Swallowed, gasped, shrieked

Jarred, flared, strained, popped

Drew, grabbed, held, gripped

Dropped, skittered

PHRASES – NOUNS AND ADJECTIVES

- ★ Out of the corner of his eye
- ★ For a moment
- ★ Only seconds before
- ★ Out of sight
- ★ Out of range
- ★ Almost at the top . . . almost safe
- ★ *Quiet as a grave*
- ★ Gust of wind
- ★ Raging waters of the lake
- ★ *Stalactites like spears*
- ★ Thick cudgel
- ★ A serpent with a diamond-shaped head
- ★ Millions of bats, like a black plume of smoke
- ★ Bulging, burning, orange eyes
- ★ *Both hands on her iron-tipped spear*

PHRASES – VERBS

- ★ By the time he had reached . . .
- ★ Felt like a trap
- ★ Couldn't back away now
- ★ *Descended a precipitous path into a huge cavern*

* Squeezed through a hole carved out of the rocky wall
* *Emerged from the passage into . . .*
* Came to a narrow archway
* Reached the stream of boiling rock
* *Ventured further in*
* Edged down the . . .
* *Put a hand on her arm*
* Indicated that they should move to either side of the pillar
* *With his arms fully extended . . .*
* Felt gingerly along the wall
* Felt along the wall for any holes in the rock
* Raised his hand to shield himself from the fiery blast of wind
* Jerked his hand back
* Threw her arms out
* Flapped his hands in front of him
* Clung to each other
* *Stopped dead in her tracks*
* Too frightened to move
* Froze, trapped in the glare of . . .
* *Crouched behind the tomb*
* Dropped to his knees behind a large rock
* Hugged the wall with her back
* Shuffled sideways along the ledge
* Stepped sideways out of the shelter of the rocks
* As he inched forward . . .
* Turned and walked backwards to check behind them
* Stepped forward to get a closer look
* Moved warily around the chamber
* Edged closer towards the source of the sound
* *Without taking his eyes from . . .*
* Stared upwards
* Peered cautiously around . . .
* Kept glancing behind her
* *Concealed in the darkness*
* Trapped in a dead end with nowhere to run
* *Whirled around*
* Crawled as fast as she could
* Scuttled backwards on his elbows
* Rolled quickly to the side
* *Quickened her pace*
* Raced down the passage
* Forced himself to move faster
* Moved fast and made for the wall of the cavern
* Sprinted to the wall

- ⋆ Darted down the slope
- ⋆ Hurtled down the slope
- ⋆ *A mistake to glance down*
- ⋆ Willed himself not to look down
- ⋆ Tried to forget that it was a long way to fall
- ⋆ *Sprung from rock to rock*
- ⋆ As he sprang off the rock . . .
- ⋆ Launched himself across the gap
- ⋆ Leapt over the crack that split like a lightning bolt
- ⋆ *With his arms fully extended . . .*
- ⋆ Rushed at the wall, arms pumping
- ⋆ Reached for the ledge
- ⋆ Clambered up the wall
- ⋆ Found footholds in the rough-hewn stones
- ⋆ *Hung in mid-air for an age*
- ⋆ Hung there, legs flailing, shoulders burning
- ⋆ Struggled to stay out of reach
- ⋆ *Just as he hit the ground . . .*
- ⋆ Threw herself forward
- ⋆ Flattened herself against . . .
- ⋆ Fell forward and sprawled on the floor
- ⋆ Flipped over onto her back
- ⋆ Sent sprays of gravel over the edge
- ⋆ Crashed onto the other side
- ⋆ Couldn't have stopped even if he had wanted to
- ⋆ *Struggled to grip on to the slippery ledge*
- ⋆ Clawed at the ground to stop himself toppling into the chasm
- ⋆ *Almost slipped*
- ⋆ Slid on the loose stones
- ⋆ Managed to keep his balance
- ⋆ Couldn't stay upright
- ⋆ Hit the ground hard
- ⋆ Arms flailed as she tried to keep her balance
- ⋆ Knocked backwards by the force of the blast
- ⋆ Thrown violently backwards
- ⋆ Sent him plummeting through the air
- ⋆ *Jarred her elbows and wrists*
- ⋆ Pain flared up her arms
- ⋆ Could feel his knuckles popping with the strain
- ⋆ Jarred every bone in his body
- ⋆ *Swallowed a couple of deep breaths*
- ⋆ Shrieked as the ground opened up behind her
- ⋆ *Avoided toppling into the chasm*
- ⋆ Landed in the raging waters of the lake below

- *Dodged the falling stone*
- Never saw the thing that seized hold of her
- Plunged from the roof
- Slid out of the tomb
- Lunged towards her
- Slammed her against the wall
- *Drew his sword*
- Drew his sword and spun on his heel
- *Struggled to get her dagger out of its sheath*
- Held the blade before him
- One hand held his shield, the other his sword
- *Descended where her head had been*
- Missed the trampling hooves by a hair's breadth
- Held the hilt of his sword tightly
- Made a grab for her sword
- Slipped out of her hand
- Threw herself after her dagger
- Sliced the vine that grasped his body
- Let his arrow fly

SENTENCES

He put a hand on her arm as he noticed a movement out of the corner of his eye.

As the hissing sound echoed off the walls of the cave, closer this time, he indicated that they should move to either side of the pillar, out of sight.

Throwing her arms out, she felt gingerly along the wall.

Suddenly, millions of bats, like a black plume of smoke, fluttered from every corner and the passage rang with the echoes of his scream as he flapped his hands in front of him.

He jerked his hand back, cold sweat trickling down his back.

He raised his hand, trying to shield himself from the intense wind being blasted at him.

She stopped dead in her tracks, staring upwards.

They clung to each other, too frightened to move.

For a moment, he froze, trapped in the glare of its bulging, burning, orange eyes.

She crouched behind the tomb, both hands on her spear.

He was concealed in the darkness, but trapped in a dead end. If the creature returned, he knew he would have nowhere to run.

Hugging the wall with her back, she shuffled sideways along the ledge, one foot crossing the other.

As he inched forward, Tom felt along the wall for any holes in the rock.

She crawled as fast as she could, ignoring the stones that scraped her knees and elbows.

All was as quiet as a grave. Rob carried his crossbow, occasionally turning and walking backwards to check behind him.

As quietly as he could, he stepped forward to get a better look.

She moved warily around the chamber to the next archway.

He edged closer, towards the source of the sound. It felt wrong, like a trap. But he couldn't back away now.

She kept glancing behind her, every muscle in her body tensed, and quickened her pace.

He came to a narrow archway and cautiously peered around it, not knowing what he was going to find on the other side.

Without taking his eyes from the deformed dwarf-like creature in front of him, he scuttled backwards on his elbows.

Rolling quickly to the side, he missed the trampling hooves by a hair's breadth.

She dodged, none too soon, as a thick cudgel descended where her head had been only seconds before.

He drew his sword and held the blade before him.

The blade slipped out of her hand; she threw herself after it. Made a grab for it. Just as another serpent slid out of the tomb and lunged towards her, she rolled to the side.

A gust of wind slammed her against the wall.

Glancing down was a mistake. Her foot almost slipped, sending sprays of gravel over the edge and into the flaming pit.

She stumbled, hitting the ground hard, jarring her elbows and wrists with a pain that flared up her arms.

His feet slipped. His arms flailed. He tried to keep his balance. Desperately, he clawed at the ground to stop himself toppling into the chasm that had opened up in front of him.

He was knocked backwards by the force of the blast. It was like the ground itself was writhing and bucking in an underground storm. He couldn't stay upright. He was thrown violently backwards.

She shrieked as the ground opened up behind her, and threw herself forward, just in time to avoid toppling into the chasm that had split the cave in two.

He could feel his knuckles popping as he struggled to grip on to the slippery ledge.

She fell forward, sprawling on the floor. Quickly, she flipped over onto her back and looked up.

Just as he hit the ground, a crack opened up beneath him, sending him plummeting through the air towards the raging waters of the lake in the cavern below.

She moved fast. Made for the wall of the cavern. Flattened herself against it. Just as she felt the stone wall at her back, stalactites like spears began to plunge from the roof.

He dodged the falling stones, and leapt over the cracks that were splitting like lightning bolts ahead of him.

He raced down the passage, one hand holding his shield, the other his sword.

As she ran, she struggled to get her dagger out of its sheath.

Almost at the top, almost safe . . . almost! He forced himself to move faster, not look down, forget that it was a long way down if he fell.

He launched himself down the slope, sliding on the loose stones, but just managing to keep his balance and surge on.

He rose to his feet, and sprinted to the wall, dropping to his knees behind a large rock.

He darted down the slope, springing from rock to rock.

He clambered up the wall, easily finding footholds in the rough-hewn stone.

Desperate, he rushed at the wall, arms pumping. He jumped. Even with his arms fully extended, only his fingertips reached the ledge. The rest of his body smashed against the stone, driving out his breath. He gasped and hung there, legs flailing, shoulders burning, as he struggled to stay out of its reach.

He swallowed a couple of deep breaths, and hurtled down the slope. By the time he had reached the stream of boiling rock, he couldn't have stopped even if he had wanted to. Panic made him take off too early, and as he sprang off the rock, he seemed to hang there for an age before he crashed onto the other side with an impact that jarred every bone in his body.

She whirled round, but never saw the thing that seized hold of her.

She drew her sword and spun on her heel. Anything could be hiding in the shadows.

Stepping sideways out of the shelter of the rocks, he let his arrow fly.

Holding the hilt of his sword tightly, he cut the vine that grasped his body.

SECTION 3 – REACTION

WORDS

Nouns	**Brain**, muscles, nerves, pins and needles, heart, throat, chest, lungs, breath, neck, arms, hands, face, mouth, lips, eyes
	Instinct, sense, sensation, images, panic, terror
	Glance, look, stare
Adjectives	**Dry**, ice-cold, gnawing, lingering
	Sixth, tingling, prickling
	Ready, determined, unwavering
	Painful, rasping, wheezing
	Trembling, quivering, shivering, shuddering
	Wide, staring, gaping
Verbs	**Wondered**, expected, knew, realised, remembered
	Alerted, warned, prepared
	Willed, prayed, hoped
	Listened, heard
	Felt, touched, brushed
	Closed, squeezed, clenched, tightened, twisted, banged, stabbed
	Rooted, nailed
	Glanced, peered, scanned, searched, tracked, probed, darted, flickered, blinked
	Shot, exchanged
	Glued, fixed, stared
	Sucked, gasped, swallowed, gulped, choked, trailed off, sawed, razed
	Twisted, dropped open, uttered, whimpered, yelled, shrieked
	Covered, clutched, pressed
	Felt, groped, floundered, flailed

PHRASES – NOUNS AND ADJECTIVES

- ★ Dark, yawning entrance to the cave
- ★ Sudden, intense brightness
- ★ *Every nerve in his body*
- ★ Every muscle in his body
- ★ Like ice-cold needles in the back of his neck
- ★ A tingling, sixth sense
- ★ *A tingling sensation that he wasn't alone*
- ★ A lingering chill
- ★ Quivering dread of an invisible presence
- ★ Fear of when it would appear again
- ★ Fear of what would happen when it did
- ★ Too terrified to look up
- ★ A thousand terrors
- ★ Terrifying images
- ★ *Out of the corner of her eye*
- ★ Wide, staring eyes
- ★ *At every new noise*
- ★ Sound of echoing footsteps
- ★ *Throat suddenly dry*
- ★ Painful gasps
- ★ *With trembling hands*
- ★ Ready for anything

PHRASES – VERBS

- ★ When she entered its gloomy depths . . .
- ★ As a shadow fell across the entrance . . .
- ★ As he turned his head . . .
- ★ As his hand brushed something in the dark . . .
- ★ As a single word roared in her head . . .
- ★ *Not sure what he expected*
- ★ Wondered what she would find when she entered . . .
- ★ Flashed through her mind
- ★ *Made him look up*
- ★ Warned him not to move
- ★ Knew he had to think of something fast
- ★ Realised she wasn't going to make it
- ★ *Alerted it to her presence*
- ★ Listened for the venomous hiss
- ★ Getting closer by the minute
- ★ Felt as if there were eyes everywhere

* Could not see it but knew it was there
* *Felt icy fingers close around her heart*
* Banged against his ribs
* Stabbed by a splinter of fear
* *Tightened and twisted*
* Clenched in panic
* *Seemed nailed to the ground*
* Fought her body's natural instinct to run
* *Glanced behind him*
* Cast one glance over her shoulder
* Peered out and squinted into the darkness
* Strained to see through the dim light
* Scanned the chamber
* Looked for a means of escape
* Searched for any sign of movement
* Tracked from side to side
* Probed the shadows at the edge of the cave
* Darted wildly back and forth
* *Kept her eyes glued to the entrance*
* Kept her narrowed eyes fixed to the floor
* Couldn't tear her gaze away from . . .
* Stared unwavering on the path before him
* *Willed himself not to look*
* Prayed that if she kept her eyes closed it would . . .
* *Flickered briefly to his face*
* Shot him a warning glance
* Exchanged a nervous look
* *Made her blink rapidly*
* Blinked the darkness out of her eyes
* *Set in a thin, determined line*
* Sucked in a breath
* Swallowed, his throat suddenly dry
* Choked back a gasp
* Trailed off as he realised what lay ahead
* Breath came in painful gasps
* Could hear his own ragged breathing
* Sawed in and out
* *Twisted in a scream that never came*
* Uttered a silent, desperate cry
* Whimpered and covered her face with her hands
* Clutched his hand to his mouth to stop himself screaming
* Uttered a thin, high-pitched scream
* Yelled at the top of his voice
* Couldn't help the shriek of terror that escaped his throat

- ⭐ Echoed through the cave
- ⭐ *Felt his way*
- ⭐ Floundered around in the dark
- ⭐ *Slithered to a halt*
- ⭐ Struggled to nock her arrow
- ⭐ Fumbled to unsheathe her sword
- ⭐ Dropped her dagger

SENTENCES

She could not help looking at the dark, yawning entrance to the cave, and wondering what she would find when she entered its gloomy depths.

He felt as if there were eyes everywhere following his every move.

He was not sure what he expected, so he was ready for anything.

Every nerve in his body warned him not to move, even though his arm was shaking and pins and needles prickled painfully in his ankle.

A tingling sixth sense made him look up. As he turned his head, he froze.

She felt icy fingers close round her heart. Her stomach tightened and twisted as a single word roared in her head.

It was a quivering dread of a presence he could not see, but knew was there.

Katie was stabbed by a splinter of fear, fear of when it would appear again, fear of what would happen when it did.

He felt his courage fading. His feet seemed nailed to the ground.

A thousand terrors flashed through her mind at once, and, with trembling hands, she struggled desperately to nock her arrow.

She tensed, fighting her body's natural instinct to run, and having to fight hard to do so.

He had a lingering chill, as if someone was pushing ice-cold needles into the back of his neck.

His stomach clenched in panic and he knew he had to think of something fast. The sound of echoing footsteps was getting closer by the minute.

His heart banging against his ribs, he squeezed through the hole and edged towards the lake.

There was a look of sheer terror on her face. She sucked in her breath as shivers racked her body.

His mouth was set in a thin line, his gaze unwavering on the path before him.

He willed himself not to look.

She prayed that if she kept her eyes closed it would go away.

His eyes tracked from side to side, probing the shadows at the edges of the cave.

Her wide eyes strained to see through the dim light and darted wildly back and forth.

The sudden intense brightness made her blink rapidly.

They kept their eyes glued to the entrance, searching for any sign of movement.

Kitty kept her narrowed eyes fixed to the floor, too terrified to look up at whatever had touched her.

Her eyes widened and her body jerked at every new noise.

Kitty's eyes flickered briefly to Robert's face and they exchanged a nervous look.

She blinked the darkness out of her eyes, trying to focus.

Frantically, she scanned the chamber, looking for a means of escape.

She cast one glance over her shoulder and realised she wasn't going to make it.

John couldn't tear his gaze away from the snake's fiery eyes.

He watched and waited. Slowly, he peered out and squinted into the darkness. His eyes darted left and right, probing for a flicker of movement.

She shot him a warning glance to keep hidden.

He kept glancing behind him, listening for the venomous hiss, every muscle in his body tensed.

It circled them warily, its eyes flicking from one to the other.

He swallowed; his throat suddenly dry.

He slithered to a halt, his breath coming in painful gasps.

She sucked in a shallow breath – a tiny sound, but a sound that alerted it to her presence.

He could hear his own ragged breathing, sawing in and out, otherwise it was silent.

Her mouth twisted in a scream that never came.

He choked back a gasp as a shadow fell across the entrance to the cave.

When she swallowed it was as if lots of tiny, needle-tipped claws were scratching at her throat.

She stopped, her mouth open, and uttered a silent, desperate cry.

He uttered a thin, high-pitched scream, which echoed through the cave.

He clutched his hand to his mouth to stop himself screaming out, but as his hand brushed against something in the dark, he threw back his head and yelled at the top of his voice.

He couldn't help the shriek of terror that escaped his throat.

7

Ruined cities

Kitty passed through the west gate and scanned the ruins. She was faced with a labyrinth of crumbling walls and pillars, courtyards and tunnels that spread out in all directions. Archways pocked every crumbling wall, like rat-holes, leading into dark alleys.

She knew it was here. She could feel it. She had the strangest feeling of being summoned by a presence, lurking in the background, but which she could never see.

She hesitated at every pillar, every arched gateway, cautiously peering around them, not knowing what she was going to find on the other side. **Every moment became an exercise in paranoia**: watching over her shoulder, jumping at every sound, sliding her hand to her sword, checking that it was still there.

All along she had had a nagging suspicion that she was delivering herself into a trap, but nothing could have prepared her for what she met around the next corner.

SECTION 1 – SETTING

WORDS

Nouns	**Hill**, hillocks, slope, terrace
	Castle, towers, buttresses, turrets, battlements, moat
	Defence, walls, barbican, gate, gateways, tunnels
	Staircase, stairs, steps
	Labyrinth, maze

Streets, courtyard, square, alleys, passageways, fountain, fire-pit

Arch, archways, pillars, columns, spire, chimneys

Church, cloister, temple

Windows, shutters, doors, hinges, walls, roof, floor, ground

Carvings, statues, gargoyles, mosaics, tiles

Griffins, ogres, serpents, baboons, ravens, crows, phoenix

Wings, feathers, talons, claws, beaks, faces

Ruins, remains, outlines, shell, base, foundations, cracks, crevices

Stones, bricks, masonry, rubble, fragments

Grass, nettles, brambles, weeds, ivy, bushes

Similes/ Metaphors
Like the skeleton of a giant creature; like a path of enormous, chipped, stone teeth; like fallen trees of monstrous stone; pocked every wall like rat-holes; gaped like open mouths; like a carcass that had been picked clean; like a gunshot

Adjectives
Large, huge, hulking, vast, enormous, immense, high, towering

Ancient, archaic

Grey, black, dark, pale

Forbidding, hostile, brooding, sinister, menacing, formidable

Ruined, dilapidated, derelict, tumbledown

Broken, chipped, cracked, crumbling

Jagged, craggy, rugged, uneven, barbed, shattered

Fading, rotting, decaying

Crooked, bent, twisting, leaning

Empty, hollow, bare, barren, desolate

Gaping, yawning, cavernous

Gruesome, ghastly, macabre

Vicious, savage, monstrous

Foul-smelling, putrid, rancid, rank

Magnificent, grand, elaborate, glittering, gleaming

Triangular, circular, rectangular

Iron, stone, brick

Verbs	**Spread**, covered, surrounded
	Weaved, twisted, looped, coiled, wound, snaked
	Rose, soared, reared, loomed
	Built, erected, constructed, carved
	Led, opened on to, connected with, bordered
	Passed, emerged, faced with, found
	Destroyed, collapsed, demolished, ravaged
	Lay, rested, situated
	Toppled, tumbled, plunged, overturned
	Smashed, crashed, crushed, splintered, snapped, shattered
	Supported, bolstered, held up, propped up
	Hung, dangled, suspended, swung, swayed
	Grew, sprouted, crept, wriggled, spilled, choked
	Perched, gripped, grasped, clutched
	Sounded, echoed

PHRASES – NOUNS AND ADJECTIVES

- ★ Once a formidable defence
- ★ *At the top of the hill*
- ★ From among the hillocks
- ★ Beyond the gate
- ★ Beyond the tunnel-like arch
- ★ From each of the four gateways
- ★ In the centre of the courtyard
- ★ Among the ruins
- ★ In some of the windows
- ★ On the floor
- ★ *Huge grey castle like a mailed fist*
- ★ Great Norman towers and frowning buttresses
- ★ Large, forbidding castle with turrets and battlements
- ★ *Towering grey walls*
- ★ Broken, city walls
- ★ Ruined wall
- ★ Shattered walls
- ★ Forbidding gateway
- ★ Iron gates
- ★ *Triangular turrets like teeth along its roof*

- Hulking, crooked, black towers and turrets
- Towers and turrets and shattered, stone staircases
- Jumble of huge, high chimneys and jagged archways
- Huge, cracked chimneys
- Immense blocks of black stone
- Shining, pale stone
- Foul-smelling moat
- Terrace upon terrace of . . .
- Huge flight of steps
- Lookout towers
- Ancient, stone towers
- Labyrinth of crumbling walls and towers, courtyards and tunnels
- *City streets*
- Magnificent courtyard
- Pillared entrance to the temple
- Empty shell of a temple
- Like the skeleton of a giant, sprawling creature
- Long row of dilapidated, stone pillars
- Towering pillars
- Crumbling columns
- Ancient cloister
- Row of arches
- Ruins of a vast arch
- Stone archway
- Clock tower
- Leaning, crooked spire
- *A succession of grotesque gargoyles*
- Gruesome griffins
- Ogres with serpent heads
- Baboons with the faces of men
- Elaborate stone carvings
- Stone statues
- Vivid, stained-glass windows
- Ornate fountain
- *Enormous phoenix*
- Gleaming tail feathers
- Vicious talons
- Outstretched wings ready for flight
- *Crumbling chimneys and hanging gutters*
- Broken stone carvings
- Crumbling bricks
- Pile of masonry
- Shattered fragments
- Piece of timber

* Part of a flight of stairs
* Like a path of enormous, chipped, stone teeth
* Like fallen trees of monstrous stone
* Cracked, fading mosaics
* *Tussocks of grass and nettles*
* Weeds and ivy
* Thorny bushes
* Barely visible through the overgrown grass
* *Hollow creak of his boot*
* Sudden bang of a shutter like a gunshot
* Flock of crows

PHRASES – VERBS

* As the sun began to set . . .
* Cast shadows over the . . .
* Cast jagged shadows along the ground
* *Spread out in all directions*
* Weaved in and out of the hillside
* Surrounded the ancient city
* *Soared into the clouds*
* Reared up out of . . .
* Built on the top of the hill
* Led up to the top of the hill
* Carved into the side of the hill
* *Passed under a crumbling archway*
* Found themselves walking down . . .
* Emerged in what had once been . . .
* Led into the centre of a courtyard
* Led into dark alleys
* Went past a pillared entrance to the temple
* Bordered the square
* Pocked with the remains of buildings
* Pocked every wall, like rat-holes
* Stood dark and empty
* Gaped like open mouths
* *All that was left was . . .*
* Could make out the jagged outlines of . . .
* Had been completely destroyed
* Had been broken off
* Toppled onto their sides
* Found broken pillars
* Held up non-existent roofs

- ☆ Lay in pieces on the ground
- ☆ Lay in piles of rubble
- ☆ Hung off their hinges
- ☆ Lay across the street
- ☆ Had collapsed on their own foundations
- ☆ Gathered at their bases
- ☆ Like a carcass that had been picked clean
- ☆ *Grown over the remains*
- ☆ Sprouted in and around them
- ☆ Eaten their way into the cracks
- ☆ Spread their tentacles into every crevice
- ☆ Crept and wriggled over the ruins
- ☆ *Carved with ravens*
- ☆ Jutted out from the towers
- ☆ Gripped the stone
- ☆ *Perched in the trees*
- ☆ Rose cawing in the air
- ☆ Echoed along the passageways

SENTENCES

Beyond the black gate that lay in pieces on the ground, a labyrinth of crumbling walls and towers, courtyards and tunnels spread out in all directions.

The broken city walls weaved in and out of the hillside, once a formidable defence surrounding the ancient city that had been built on top of the hill.

From among the hillocks that had grown over the remains of the ancient city, they could see the empty shell of the temple like the skeleton of a giant creature whose carcass had been picked clean.

A huge flight of steps led up to the top of the hill, past a pillared entrance to the temple at the top. The hill was pocked with the remains of buildings – terrace above terrace of jagged archways, ancient stone towers and crumbling columns.

From each of the four gateways, a stone archway carved with ravens led into the centre of the courtyard.

The ruins of a vast arch, a long row of stone pillars, and walls that held up non-existent roofs were all that was left.

They passed under a crumbling archway that had broken stone carvings jutting out of the walls, and emerged in what had once been a magnificent, pillared courtyard.

Hulking, crooked towers and turrets, built from immense blocks of black stone, soared into the clouds. In some of the windows, he could make out the jagged outlines of what remained of elaborate stained-glass windows.

Beyond the tunnel-like arch were the city streets where the buildings stood dark and empty.

Ruined walls, now a pile of masonry, bordered the square. Trees grew in and around them. A flock of crows that had been perched in the trees rose cawing into the air as they entered.

Some of the towering pillars had collapsed on their own foundations, their shattered fragments gathered at the bases like felled trees of monstrous stone. Tussocks of grass and nettles grew in and around them.

Many of the columns had been broken off, and had toppled onto their sides. It was like walking along a path of enormous, chipped, stone teeth.

A succession of grotesque, broken gargoyles – snarling griffins, ogres with heads of baboons, monkeys with the faces of men – jutted out from the towers, casting jagged shadows along the ground.

In the centre of the courtyard was an elaborate fountain. Rearing up out of the dry interior was a phoenix, its enormous outstretched wings ready for flight, gleaming tail feathers trailing behind it, vicious talons gripping the stone.

As the sun began to set, the pillars cast shadows over the cracked, fading mosaics on the floor.

Among the ruins, he found broken pillars made of shining pale stone.

Sections of the wall had come away and lay in piles of rubble, one of the towers had been completely destroyed, and the solid iron gates hung off their hinges. A piece of timber lay across the street from him – part of a flight of stairs.

Weeds and ivy had eaten their way into the cracks of the ruins and spread their tentacles into every crevice.

Archways pocked every wall, like rat-holes, leading into dark alleys, where doors gaped like open mouths.

In the silence, the sudden bang of a shutter cracked like a gunshot.

The hollow creak of his boots echoed along the pavement and passageways.

SECTION 2 – INTERACTION

WORDS	
Nouns	**City**, ruins, archway, alley, courtyard, dead end
	Gate, gateway, walls, columns, roof, roof-edge, tiles, door, doorway
	Slope, corner, side, edge, ledge, gap, crack

Shell, rubble, masonry, stones, rocks, boulders

Movement, sound, noise, whinny

Danger, threat

Dark, gloom, shadows

Hitching post, horse, flanks, head, neck, ears, nostrils, saddle, reins

Legs, feet, knees, ankles, heels, eyes, stomach

Sword, hilt, blade

Similes/ Metaphors

As nimbly as a mountain goat; *toppled like a felled oak*

Adjectives

Magnificent, majestic, grand

Empty, bare, desolate

Gaping, yawning

Jagged, uneven, rough-hewn

Crumbling, decaying, collapsing

Flickering, jerking

Quiet, stealthy, furtive, skulking, cautious, uneasy

Quick, swift

Creeping, squirming

High, shrill, piercing

Terrified, petrified, frantic

Crunching, grinding, pounding

Verbs

Thought, summoned, controlled

Felt, sensed

Saw, looked, watched, searched, gazed, peered, glanced, stared

Listened, heard

Entered, ventured, came to, emerged

Backed away, retreated, hugged, pressed

Shuffled, edged, inched, eased

Lay, rolled, writhed, twisted, crawled

Dodged, ducked, dived

Struck, hit

Stopped, paused, waited, straightened

Turned, spun, swung, whirled

Ran, darted, sprinted, dashed, charged

Blundered, staggered, slipped, slid, fell, toppled

Bent, sprung, leapt, pushed off, jumped

Climbed, clambered, scaled, scampered

Scattered, bounded

Groped, flailed, flung

Drew, clutched, held

Rode, trotted, galloped

Grabbed, yanked, jerked, hauled, gripped, dug, slapped, urged

Stirred, whinnied, shied, reared

Mounted, dismounted, tied, tethered

PHRASES – NOUNS AND ADJECTIVES

- ★ For almost an hour
- ★ Out of the corner of her eye
- ★ *On the roof*
- ★ Directly above him
- ★ Far beneath his feet
- ★ By the gate
- ★ At the end of the alley
- ★ On the other side
- ★ Over the edge
- ★ Another dead end
- ★ *Centre of the city*
- ★ Tunnel-like archway
- ★ Magnificent courtyard
- ★ *Empty shell*
- ★ Piles of jagged masonry
- ★ Rusty hinges
- ★ *No one there*
- ★ Every flickering movement
- ★ *As nimble as a mountain goat*
- ★ In one swift movement
- ★ *Ears back, nostrils quivering*

PHRASES – VERBS

* Tried to control the creeping terror
* Summoned up his courage
* *Thought he saw . . .*
* *As he turned . . .*
* As she rode into . . .
* Trotted quietly around the . . .
* *Entered cautiously*
* Made a gradual, skulking progress
* Ventured a step closer . . . then another
* *Came to a gateway*
* Emerged in what had once been . . .
* *Backed away*
* Stepped further into the shadows
* Hugged the jagged, crumbling wall
* Shuffled sideways
* *Lay on her stomach*
* Crawled to the roof-edge
* Writhed and twisted
* Crawled through the gaps in the crumbling columns
* *Spun on her heels and checked behind her*
* Dodged out of sight
* Dived head first
* Ducked and dived behind . . .
* Flung himself down behind . . .
* Struck the ground in a tuck
* Rolled to his feet
* *Stopped dead in her tracks*
* Straightened. Listened. Peered towards . . .
* Paused at the . . .
* *Turned and ran*
* Darted down the slope
* Sprinted down the alley
* Charged through the gaping doorway
* Broke into a stumbling run
* Blundered and slipped
* Darted and dodged through the ruins
* Sprung from rock to rock, boulder to boulder
* *Faced with another collapsed wall*
* Blocked the entrance to the courtyard
* Saw it was a dead end
* Tried to back out of the alley
* *Took a massive leap of faith*

- Ran for the wall of rocks
- Bent his knees
- Leapt upwards
- Pushed off the ground and jumped upwards
- Clambered to the safety of the rooftops
- Clambered up the outer walls
- Found footholds in the rough-hewn stone
- Scaled the crumbling walls
- *Scampered across the rooftops*
- Leaped across the gaps
- Threw himself at . . . and clung on
- Feet flailed in the air
- Wondered if he'd misjudged his leap
- As the . . . rose to meet him . . .
- Had almost reached . . . when . . .
- *Slid under his feet*
- Cascaded beneath his feet
- Sent fragments of stone
- Scattered the rubble and loose stones
- Bounded away into the dark
- *Almost slipped*
- Staggered slightly
- Felt his ankle shoot out from under him
- Toppled like a felled oak
- Stumbled and flung his hand out in front of him
- Groped for something to stop him falling
- *When he looked . . .*
- As he looked around . . .
- Swung his head from side to side
- Gazed around with darting eyes
- Peered down
- Peered around the gateway
- Stared upwards
- Peered into the gloom
- Gaze froze on something in front of her
- *Searched for a way out*
- Did not look back
- Did not know what he was going to find
- Glancing down was a mistake
- *Sensed danger*
- As she drew her sword . . .
- Clutched the hilt of his sword
- Held his blade before him
- *Grabbed the horse's reins*

* Swung himself up into the saddle
* *Horse stirred uneasily*
* Gave a high, terrified whinny
* Shied and reared
* *As he dug his heels into the horse's flanks...*
* Had to grip tightly with his knees
* Stopped herself being thrown from the saddle
* *Slapped his horse's neck*
* Urged it through the gates
* Galloped to the closest building
* *Jerked her horse to a stop*
* Hauled their horses to a halt
* *Jumped from the saddle*
* Dismounted and tethered his horse
* *Heard a crunching noise*

SENTENCES

He noticed her gaze slip upwards past his head. Out of the corner of his eye, as he turned, he thought he saw a flicker of movement by the gate, as if someone was dodging out of sight. But when he looked, there was no one there.

They trotted quietly around the city and entered it cautiously.

As she rode into the centre of the city, her horse stirred uneasily, ears back, nostrils quivering. Suddenly, one of the horses gave a high, terrified whinny, and shied, rearing. Kitty had to grip tightly with her knees to stop herself being thrown from the saddle.

He ducked, and dived behind a pillar for cover.

Tom flung himself down behind the fountain.

John charged through the gaping doorway. Diving head first, he struck the ground in a tuck and rolled to his feet, sword at the ready.

For almost an hour, he dodged and hid, making a gradual skulking progress through the ruined city, jumping at every slight sound, every flickering movement.

Lying on her stomach, she crawled to the roof-edge and peered down.

As nimbly as a mountain goat, he clambered to the safety of the rooftops, scaling the crumbling walls, and scampered across them, leaping over the gaps.

Rob clambered up the outer walls, easily finding footholds in the rough-hewn stone.

Bending his knees, he leapt upwards in one swift movement.

She ran for the wall of rocks, pushed off the ground and jumped upwards.

He'd almost reached the next level, when the surface slid under his feet. He threw himself at the next ledge and clung on. Stones cascaded beneath his feet. As he pulled himself to safety, another stone bounded away into the dark.

Summoning up his courage, he took a massive leap of faith. Piles of jagged masonry glinted in the moonlight far beneath his feet as they flailed in the air.

As the hard grey wall rose up to meet him, he wondered if he'd misjudged his leap. But, suddenly, he was on the roof, staggering slightly, but still on his feet.

He sensed danger and leapt to his feet, drawing his sword.

A shadow darted ahead. He jumped and drew his sword.

The door was pushed open, the rusty hinges screeching. He clutched the longsword in both hands.

He clutched the hilt of his sword and gazed around with darting eyes.

Katie stopped dead in her tracks, staring upwards.

He straightened. Listened. Peered towards the empty shell that had once been the temple.

Trying to control the creeping terror that was spreading through her, she paused at the tunnel-like archway, and peered into the gloom.

Slowly, he slid forward. He was about to extend his hand when he heard a crunching noise directly above him.

Hugging the jagged, crumbling wall with her back, she shuffled sideways.

Writhing and twisting, Katie crawled through the gaps in the crumbling columns and emerged in what had once been a magnificent pillared courtyard.

He came to a gateway and cautiously peered around it, not knowing what he was going to find on the other side.

She ventured a step closer. Then another.

He backed away. Looked around. As he did so, his gaze froze on something behind Katie.

Anything could be hiding in the shadows. As she drew her sword, she spun on her heels and checked behind her.

He drew his sword. Held the blade before him. Moved further into the shadows, scattering the rubble and loose stones.

Glancing down was a mistake. Her foot almost slipped, sending fragments of stone over the edge.

He stumbled and flung his hand out in front of him, groping for something to stop him falling.

Tom felt his ankles shoot out from under him and he toppled like a felled oak.

He darted down the slope, springing from rock to rock.

Desperately, he broke into a stumbling run.

He turned and ran and did not look back.

Blundering and slipping, he leapt from boulder to boulder, darting and dodging through the ruins.

She sprinted down the alley. At the end, she was faced with another collapsed wall that blocked the entrance to the courtyard. Another dead end.

He started to make his way towards the sound when a shadow moved behind him; something was raised above his head.

He slipped into a narrow passageway, and saw it was a dead end. He tried to back out, but the entrance was already blocked. He swung his head from side to side, searching for a way out, but there was none.

As he dug his heels into the horse's flanks, he slapped its neck and urged it through the gates.

Katie galloped to the closest building, and as she jerked her horse to a halt, she jumped from the saddle.

He grabbed the horse's reins and swung himself up into the saddle.

He dismounted and tethered his horse to a hitching post.

SECTION 3 – REACTION

WORDS

Nouns   **Sense**, sensation, instinct, urge

Paranoia, paralysis

Dread, horror, fear, unease

Courage, bravery, determination

Nerves, mind, panic, breath, adrenalin, sweat

Threats, traps, trouble, danger, evil, menace

Face, skin, neck, throat, windpipe, eyes, spine, hands, fingers

Body, heart, ribs, shoulders, legs, forehead, stomach

Alley, door, doorway, roof

Boulders, pillars, columns, rubble

Night, gloom, darkness, shadows, shapes

Dagger, sword, bow, weapon

Cuts, bruises, blood, pain

Similes/ Metaphors	*Jangled together like wind chimes*

Adjectives

Huge, enormous

Shattered, smashed, cracked, splintered

Fierce, evil, menacing, sinister

Cold, chilly, icy

Spider-like, tingling, prickling

Wide, bulging

Staring, gaping

Several, numerous, countless

Possible, potential, likely

Underlying

Quick, rapid, fleeting

Wild, frantic

Strange, odd, curious, eerie, suspicious

Shifting, moving, flitting

Verbs

Felt, thought, wondered, warned, knew, realised

Happened, occurred, took place

Acted, moved

Lay, settled down

Crawled, jangled, prickled, tingled

Jolted, kick-started

Raced, pounded, hammered, jumped

Gasped, choked, caught

Saw, made out, looked, watched, peered, scanned, strained, probed, glanced, flickered, darted

Gripped, clutched, drew

Stumbled, smashed, struggled

Winded, bruised, cut, hurt, injured

PHRASES – NOUNS AND ADJECTIVES

* Every waking moment
* *In front of him*
* Behind her
* Behind every boulder, every pillar
* Behind the huge boulders of shattered columns
* Through every gaping doorway
* On the edge of the roof
* *A menacing presence*
* A fierce gust
* Sound of footsteps
* *With a sudden feeling of dread*
* Uneasy about what lay ahead
* Certain there was someone or something
* As if some sense at the back of her mind
* Cold, spider-like sensation
* A tight knot in the pit of her stomach
* An explosion of adrenalin
* *All the colour from his face*
* The skin on the back of his neck
* Wide, staring eyes
* *Numerous cuts*
* Trickle of warm blood
* Pain in his . . .
* All the warning she had
* Only a second in which to act

PHRASES – VERBS

* As soon as he had entered the ruins . . .
* As a shadow fell across the entrance . . .
* As a shadow rose out of the darkness . . .
* As night approached and the shadows lengthened . . .
* When he stood . . .
* *Beginning to feel a great unease*
* Saw potential threats and traps behind every . . .
* Wondered what she would find when she . . .
* Warned that she was walking into trouble
* Could not help looking at . . .
* Fought back the urge to flee
* Forced herself to find the courage to . . .
* Put one foot in front of the other

- *Fought an underlying sense of panic*
- Became an exercise in paranoia
- *Trying to tell her something*
- Something she did not realise she knew
- *Knew his life hung by a thread*
- Realised her mistake too late
- Several things happened at once
- *Crawled down her spine*
- Moved to her fingers
- Jangled together like wind chimes
- Felt a cold sweat break out on . . .
- Prickled as he entered
- *Felt evil*
- Felt full of dark secrets
- Lurking in the shadows
- *Raced through her body*
- Hammered against his ribs
- *Watched over their shoulders*
- Jumped at every sound
- *Peered through . . .*
- Scanned the gloom
- Strained to pierce the darkness
- Probed the ruins
- Turned to look in the direction of . . .
- Glanced rapidly around
- Flickered from . . . to . . .
- Darted wildly from side to side
- Began to make out strange, shifting shapes
- Scanned the narrow, darkened alleys
- *Took his breath away*
- Snaked around his windpipe
- Choked his breath into shallow gasps
- Caught in his throat
- *Stumbled and smashed into a pile of rubble*
- Struggled to his feet
- *Jolted him out of his paralysis*
- Kick-started his survival instincts
- Had to hang on
- Had to claw his way to the top
- *Winded and bruised*
- Made his leg buckle
- Dripped down from his forehead
- *Gripped her dagger tighter*
- Hands dropped to their weapons at the slightest sound

SENTENCES

She was beginning to feel a great unease about what lay ahead, as if some sense at the back of her mind was trying to tell her something she had not realised she knew.

He saw potential threats and traps behind every boulder, every pillar, through every gaping doorway.

She could not help looking at the dark, yawning entrance to the temple and wondering what she would find when she entered its crumbling, gloomy depths.

A cold, spider-like sensation crawled down her spine. The prickling sensation moved to her fingers. She felt a cold sweat break out above her upper lip.

A tight knot in the pit of her stomach warned Gail that she was walking into trouble. Shuddering, she fought back the urge to flee.

The skin on the back of his neck prickled as he entered the courtyard. The place felt evil, as if a menacing presence was lurking in the shadows.

An explosion of adrenalin raced through her body and she quickened her pace.

As he glanced back, his heart almost stopped.

She forced herself to find the courage to put one foot in front of the other.

As soon as he had entered the ruins, he'd been fighting an underlying sense of panic, and as night approached and the shadows lengthened, the ruins suddenly felt full of dark secrets.

Every waking moment became an exercise in paranoia: watching over their shoulders, jumping at every sound, hands dropping to their weapons if a horse so much as snorted.

All the colour had drained from her face.

Her wide, staring eyes scanned the ruins.

She peered through the gaping door, and gripped her dagger tighter. She was still scouring the gloom when her lantern flickered. The light wavered again . . . then went out.

He turned to look in the direction in which she was staring.

Glancing rapidly round, his eyes flicked from the fountain to the archway.

His wide eyes strained to pierce the darkness and darted wildly from side to side, certain there was someone or something behind the huge boulders of the shattered columns.

She settled down on her stomach on the edge of the roof and scanned the narrow alleys.

He choked back a gasp as a shadow fell across the entrance.

Panic snaked around his windpipe and choked his breath into shallow gasps.

His breath caught in his throat as a shadow rose out of the darkness in front of him.

She stumbled and smashed into a pile of rubble, winded and bruised and bleeding from numerous cuts.

He struggled to his feet, his right arm bruised and cut.

A trickle of warm blood dripped down from his forehead and into his mouth. It jolted him out of his paralysis and kick-started his survival instincts. He had to hang on. He had to claw his way to the top. And quick.

When he stood, the pain in his knee made his leg buckle.

8

Castles

THE S/C-I-R STRUCTURE

As the sun peeped over the horizon, the drawbridge came creaking down. The sound of oiled chains shattered the early morning silence as the portcullis was slowly drawn up.

Tom kicked his horse's flanks and rode towards the entrance, his eyes scanning the battlements for any sign of movement, any tell-tale glint of metal. The sound of his horse's hooves clattering over the open drawbridge seemed deafening, as if they were announcing his arrival.

Tom glanced up again. **He couldn't see anything, but sensed they were waiting. They were expecting him. Fear of what was to come sharpened his senses and made him alive to every detail. A bead of sweat trickled from his brow** as he spotted the gruesome row of severed heads sprouting from poles planted above the gates.

Tightening his grip on the reins, Tom urged his horse forward and rode through the gates. **He could almost feel the crossbows aimed at his back. Even though his heart was pounding, he knew he could not afford to make any mistakes now. He tried to swallow his fear but his mouth had suddenly gone dry.**

As Rob walked past the gatehouse, **his back quivered with the strain of maintaining a steady walk when every instinct demanded that he break into a desperate sprint**.

Suddenly, he stopped dead in his tracks. Behind him, he had heard the clink of spears and the faint metallic slither of chain mail. He glanced quickly over his shoulder and ducked into the shadows as the guards strode from the gatehouse.

Rob glimpsed a flicker of movement out of the corner of his eye, but he didn't have time to lift his shield. He only had seconds to register the shadow of the raised weapon before it descended to club him behind the ear. With a cry at the sudden, searing pain, he fell senseless to the ground.

SECTION 1 – SETTING

WORDS	
Nouns	**Castle**, citadel, fortress, fortification
	Cliffs, woods, trees
	Wall, curtain wall, moat, sewage
	Drawbridge, portcullis, barbican, gate, gatehouse, doors, postern, sally port
	Watchtower, towers, spires, turrets, battlements, tunnels, courtyards, dungeons
	Buildings, stables, forges, kitchen, bakery, brewery
	Windows, slits
	Gargoyles, heads, skeletons
	Staircase, stairs
	Corridor, passage, room, gallery
	Hall, platform, dais, tables, benches
	Ceiling, beams, panel
	Tapestries, animal pelts, antlers, skulls
	Battles, hunts, dog, monster, serpent
	Lights, torches, torchlight, candles, braziers, lamps
	Fire, hearth, cauldron, spit, meat, ale
	Floor, rushes, herbs, lime
	Horses, hooves, harness, flanks, reins, snort, whinny
	Soldiers, warriors, guards, sentries, archers
	Crossbows, longbows, swords, shields, knives, maces, axes, spears, war-hammers, pikes, halberds, armour
	Stands, racks, hooks
	Thud, crash, barks, boots
Similes/ Metaphors	*Like a mailed fist; cut the air like a knife*

Adjectives	**Blank**, grey, black, dark, gloomy
	Ancient, medieval
	Grim, desolate, bleak, stark, forbidding, brooding, sinister, mysterious
	Grotesque, gruesome, monstrous, hideous, macabre
	Sheer, steep, vertical
	Big, large, huge, vast, enormous, high, towering, great, massive
	Thick, dense, heavy, solid, hulking
	Long, short, thin, narrow, little
	Arched, rounded, domed, beamed, vaulted
	Smoke-blackened
	Pointed, spiked, barbed, sharp, razor-sharp
	Crooked, twisted, winding, spiral
	Carved, sculpted, chiselled
	Central, inner, left-hand, right-hand
	Stone, wooden, oak, metal, iron
	Tallow, wax, beeswax
	Hollow, echoing
	Chill, cold, icy
	Rancid, rank, foul, putrid
	Two-headed, many-headed, severed
	Armoured, iron-clad
	Roasting, baking, cooking
	Faint, quiet, muted, muffled, stifled
	Distant, far-off, faraway
	Grinding, tinkling, hissing
	Harsh, grating, rasping, jangling
	Glowing, burning, flickering, shifting, dancing
Verbs	**Built**, perched
	Rose, soared
	Surrounded, overlooked, stretched
	Brooded, loomed, thrust

Protected, lined, studded, topped, spiked, impaled

Manned, guarded, protected

Positioned, set, located, situated

Raised, drew up, opened

Close, shut, lowered, sealed, barred, slammed

Flanked, bordered, edged

Emerged, entered, went through

Covered, filled, displayed, propped

Hung, draped, dangled, adorned

Strewed, scattered, spread

Wafted, drifted

Lit, glowed, pierced

Polished, varnished, waxed

Burned, hissed, sputtered, guttered

Wielded, brandished, flourished

Rode, trotted, cantered, dismounted, tethered

Clattered, clanked, rattled

PHRASES – NOUNS AND ADJECTIVES

* On top of sheer black cliffs
* Above the woods
* Through a break in the trees
* Behind the curtain walls
* Outside the walls
* On all sides
* By the castle gates
* Behind the jaws of the portcullis
* Either side of the doors
* In front of them
* In the middle of the otherwise blank wall
* Only thing visible above the fortifications
* *Ancient castle*
* Huge monstrosity
* Dark, brooding castle
* Grey, forbidding castle
* Vast, towering fortress

- Big, dark and mysterious
- Gloomy and deserted
- A desolate fortress in a barren, desolate land
- *Rancid, dry moat*
- Stench of sewage
- *Long, pointed, crooked spires as sharp as needles*
- Grey stone labyrinth
- Walls and towers, courtyards and tunnels
- Hulking towers and turrets
- Forbidding towers
- Thick walls
- Grim, grey walls
- *Seconds before the ...*
- Until at last she ...
- As the grinding noise of hidden cogs ...
- *Open drawbridge*
- Portcullis down
- Great gates
- An enormous, black gate
- *Another gate in an inner wall*
- Great, arched gatehouse
- *Massive, heavy doors*
- Two, massive, oak doors
- Heavy wooden door
- The thin, dark rectangle of the sally port
- A little door in a turret
- Doors to the chambers
- Through an inner door
- Barely wide enough for a single man
- *Hollow slits*
- Large, arrow-slit windows
- *Succession of grotesque gargoyles of two-headed dogs*
- Gruesome row of severed heads of executed criminals
- *On the far side of the courtyard*
- Vast paved courtyard
- Mass of smaller buildings
- Smiths' forges and stables
- Kitchens, bakery and brewery
- Smell of yeast and brewing ale
- *Several, spiral staircases*
- Down a flight of stairs
- *At the far end of the room*
- Along a passageway
- Short, unlit corridor

- On either side of the passage
- Somewhere down the passage
- *At one end of the hall*
- Down the length of the hall
- Behind the dais
- *Harsh, chill, stone hall*
- Large with a beamed ceiling
- Large room with heavy beams on the ceiling
- Smoke-blackened beams
- Magnificent carvings on the beams and panels
- Great fire with extra logs by the side of the hearth
- Stone floor
- Raised platform
- Dais with a table for the nobles
- *Even in daytime . . .*
- Tallow candles
- Dim light
- In the flickering torchlight
- Lights in the castle windows
- At regular intervals
- Around the walls
- *Armoured soldiers*
- Points of the guards' lances
- *Animal pelts and antlers*
- Large display of pikes and halberds
- Armour – mail, plate and leather
- Crossbows, longbows, shields, swords, knives, axes and maces
- Enormous skulls, spears and war-hammers
- *Smell of roasting meat*
- Huge cauldron
- *Big enough to stand in*
- *Faint tinkling of harness*
- Horses snorting and whinnying
- Soft thud of horses' hooves
- Distant cacophony of barks
- *Echo of boots*
- Clatter of swords

PHRASES – VERBS

- Had been built on a high hill
- Surrounded by a dense wood
- Brooded over the little town

* Perched on a massive, table-like rock
* Overlooking the sea
* Had been built around . . .
* *Loomed into sight*
* Thrust like a mailed fist
* Soared into the clouds
* Rose at each corner
* Stretched in all directions
* *Protected by twelve-foot-thick walls*
* Ran a dry moat
* Lined with iron spikes
* Studded with spikes
* Topped with rows of sharp, metal spikes
* Impaled anyone who attempted to charge it
* Rumoured to contain . . .
* Contained skeletons of those who had attempted to escape
* Manned by sentries with loaded crossbows
* *As they rode towards the entrance . . .*
* Set in an arched medieval portal
* Positioned between two large towers
* As the portcullis was drawn up . . .
* Clattered over the drawbridge
* Sealed shut for the night
* Shut and barred
* *Studded with huge, spiked rivets*
* Sprouted from poles planted above the gates
* Set within the left-hand door
* Reached the postern gate
* *Found themselves in . . .*
* Emerged in a central courtyard
* Reached the inner courtyard
* Dismounted and tethered their horses to an iron ring
* *Gargoyles jutted out from the corner of the tower*
* Bared their razor-sharp teeth
* *As his eyes grew accustomed to the dark . . .*
* Flickered on top of the ramparts
* Showed from a doorway
* Moved in the glow of the braziers
* Flanked by hissing torches
* Hung on metal rings around the walls
* Braziers glowed in the darkness
* Threw shifting pools of light
* Cast dancing shadows on the ground
* Pierced the gloom

- *Started to lower the portcullis*
- Slammed closed
- Slowly drew open
- *Guarded the gates*
- Stepped out, wielding lances
- Filled with pointing arrows
- Went through many passages
- Passed through a polished gallery
- On one side of her was . . .
- On the other was . . .
- *Big enough to stand in*
- Burned in the huge fireplace
- Braziers filled with burning coals
- Guttered in dishes on the tables
- *Hung with battle pennants and ancient arms*
- Strewn with rushes mixed with herbs
- Filled with long benches and trestle tables
- Arranged in two parallel lines
- Where the lord and his family sat with honoured guests
- *Covered one of the walls*
- Hung on the walls
- *Giant, ape-like monster rising from the swamp*
- Depicted hunting scenes
- Fighting a many-headed serpent
- *Piled in the corner*
- Lined with shields, swords and hauberks of every size
- Displayed in carved, wooden stands
- Propped in racks against the walls
- *Hung over an open fire*
- Stood beside a large, open fireplace
- Turned a large piece of meat on a spit
- Carried pitchers of ale to the tables
- Wafted across from the open door
- *Kicked the flanks of his horse*
- Urged his horse to move faster
- *Yelled for them to wait*
- Clashed against stones in the courtyard
- Heard voices, scuffling, grunting
- A door crashed
- *Broke the silence*
- Cut the night like a knife
- Filled the air
- Sounded in the distance
- Clanged out somewhere

SENTENCES

The castle had been built on a high hill, surrounded by a dense wood.

The ancient castle brooded over the little town, a huge monstrosity in comparison with the rest of the city.

The dark, macabre castle was perched on a massive, table-like rock on top of sheer black cliffs overlooking the sea.

A vast, towering fortress reared out of the hills.

The castle was big, dark and mysterious, with thick walls where sentries stood guard and forbidding towers – a desolate fortress in a desolate land.

The castle was the only thing visible over the fortifications. It was protected by twelve-foot-thick walls, and a rancid, dry moat lined with iron spikes, which was rumoured to contain the skeletons of those who had attempted to escape.

A grey, forbidding castle loomed into sight through a break in the trees, thrusting like a mailed fist above the woods, its hulking towers and turrets soaring into the clouds.

Outside the walls ran a dry moat studded with spikes.

Watchtowers rose at each corner, manned by sentries with loaded crossbows.

The castle had four circular towers and an enormous, black gate, topped with rows of sharp, metal spikes to impale anyone who attempted to charge it.

The castle had been built around a vast, paved courtyard, with the great grey walls of the castle rising on all four sides.

Behind the curtain walls was a mass of smaller buildings, including smiths' forges, stables, kitchens, bakery and brewery.

It was a grey stone labyrinth of walls and towers, courtyards and tunnels spreading out in all directions.

The towers had long, crooked spires as sharp as needles.

An open drawbridge led to the gate, which was positioned between two large towers.

The drawbridge came creaking down and they heard the sound of chains as the portcullis was drawn up.

As they rode towards the entrance, the hooves clattered over the open drawbridge and they emerged in the central courtyard, where they dismounted and tethered their horses to an iron ring set in the wall.

The drawbridge was up, the portcullis down, and the great gates sealed for the night, but torches flickered on top of the ramparts, and there were lights in the castle windows. Soldiers moved in the glow of braziers by the castle gates.

Just as they came within sight of the portcullis, it started to descend. Yelling for them to wait, he kicked the flanks of his horse, urging it to move faster, and burst through the entrance seconds before the gateway slammed closed.

The gate was flanked by hissing torches, which cast dancing shadows on the ground in front of them. The grinding noise of hidden cogs broke the silence and the doors were slowly shut.

Behind the jaws of the portcullis, armoured soldiers stepped out of the sentry posts, wielding lances.

The hollow slits either side of the doors were filled with pointing arrows.

Fierce-looking warriors guarded the gates, the points of their lances glittering in the moonlight.

They went inside through two massive, oak doors set in an arched medieval portal.

They found themselves in a great, arched gatehouse – the enormous, black doors were shut and barred. The doors were massive, heavy, and studded with huge, spiked rivets.

A gruesome row of the severed heads of executed criminals sprouted from poles planted above the gates.

The sally port was set within the left-hand door, a thin, dark rectangle barely wide enough for a man to pass through.

They reached the postern gate, a small, but heavy wooden door, in the middle of the otherwise blank wall.

Jutting out from the corner of the tower were a succession of grotesque gargoyles of two-headed dogs, their razor-sharp teeth bared menacingly.

They emerged in another courtyard, larger than the first, gloomy and deserted.

He was led into the courtyard, where another gate was set in an inner wall.

She went through many passages, up several spiral staircases, until at last she went through to a little door in a turret, where the battlements were on one side of her and on the other side, a steep roof.

He passed through a polished gallery, with large arrow-slit windows on one side and doors to the chambers on the other.

Through an inner door was a long, stone-flagged passage, and on either side of the passage were heavy, wooden doors.

She headed for the spiral staircase at the far end of the room.

The walls of the spiral staircase were peppered with window slits for the archers. She glanced through the arrow slit of the thick wall, and spotted a group of riders cantering towards the castle.

The spiral staircase twisted to the right so that the soldiers defending the stairs had room to swing their swords or thrust pikestaffs at advancing intruders.

They were taken along a passageway and down a flight of stairs, where he unlocked a narrow, oak door and they slid into a small, dimly lit chamber.

The hall was large, with a beamed ceiling from which hung huge banners.

It was a large room with heavy beams on the ceiling, and a fireplace at the far end big enough to stand in.

It was a harsh, chill, stone hall, with smoke-blackened beams and hung with battle pennants and ancient arms.

They entered a large hall with a high, vaulted ceiling and magnificent carvings on the beams and panels. A great fire burned in the huge fireplace. Extra logs lay by the side, warming before they could be set on the hearth.

The hall had a stone floor strewn with rushes that had been mixed with herbs. It was filled with long benches and trestle tables arranged in two parallel lines down the length of the hall. Tallow candles guttered in dishes on the tables.

At one end of the hall was a dais with a table on it, where the lord and his family sat, along with honoured guests. Behind the dais were a number of large tapestries depicting hunting scenes.

Benches sat in little clusters around braziers filled with glowing coals.

On one of the walls was a huge, medieval tapestry of a scene from Beowulf, with a giant, ape-like monster rising out of the swamp.

A tapestry of soldiers fighting a many-headed serpent covered one of the walls. On other walls, there were tapestries of great and bloody battles. Weapons were piled in the corner, crossbows, longbows, swords, knives and maces.

The walls were lined with shields, swords and hauberks of every size, knives, crossbows, maces and axes. Arrows were displayed on carved wooden stands.

Enormous skulls, spears, swords, maces and war-hammers hung on steel hooks. There was also armour – mail, plate and leather.

The walls were decorated with an array of animal pelts and antlers.

Leading out from the hall was a short, unlit corridor, with a large display of pikes and halberds propped in racks against the walls.

The smell of roasting meat wafted across from the open door.

A huge cauldron hung over an open fire.

A servant stood beside the large open fireplace, turning a large piece of meat on a spit. Other servants carried pitchers of ale to the tables.

As his eyes grew accustomed to the light, he made out a display of severed hands mounted above the door.

One of the servants lit the torches that hung in metal rings around the walls.

Even in daytime, the corridors were dark. At regular intervals around the walls were braziers that glowed in the darkness.

Lamps threw shifting pools of light to pierce the gloom.

A dim light showed from a doorway on the far side of the courtyard.

There was a sound of bolts quickly being drawn.

He heard the faint tinkling of harness, and then the soft thud of horses' hooves, which became a clatter as the soldiers rode into the courtyard.

He heard voices, scuffling and grunting. Then silence. Somewhere down the passage a door crashed.

A scream cut the night like a knife.

A distant cacophony of barks sounded in the distance.

As the portcullis jerked upwards, he heard horses snorting and whinnying, the clatter of swords in the flickering torchlight.

A gate clanged open somewhere, and the echo of boots marching on a stone floor filled the air.

SECTION 2 – INTERACTION

WORDS

Nouns	**Castle**, battlements, embrasure, rampart, parapet
	Tower, gatehouse, courtyard, stables
	Roof, tiles, walls, window, corridor, passage, stairs, hall, dais, platform, chamber
	Portcullis, wheel, gate, door, lever, rope, bolts, ring, handle
	Lists, joust, pavilion, gallery, stands, pennants, banners, arms
	Herald, pages, squires, knights, lords, ladies, nobles, crowd, villagers, servants
	Tabards, armour, chain mail, helmet, visor, slit
	Colour, background
	Sounds, noise, cacophony, cheer, shouts, groans, murmurs

Drums, trumpets, bugles, horn

Clink, slither, clatter, clank, blast

Signal, alarm, footsteps, guard, sentry, warrior, archer

Quintain, shield, bag, counterweight

Pole, ring, circle, target

Horse, mount, charger, destrier, legs, stride, hooves, flanks, neck

Saddle, harness, reins

Trot, canter, gallop, charge

Ground, track, earth, dirt, dust, clods

Thud, blow, strike, impact

Lance, spear, axe, sword, hilt, blade, knife, dagger, sheath, scabbard, belt

Bow, arrow, quarrel, bolt, groove, string, cords, tip

Back, shoulder, stomach, ribs, chest, side, legs, feet, head, forehead, eyes

Shadow, silhouette, light

Similes/ Metaphors	***Like a hammer blow***; *like a statue; like a wooden eye mocking him; as silently as a cat; in a deadly rain of wood and steel; gripped his lance like a vice*
Adjectives	**Vivid**, brightly coloured, gleaming, flaming
	Red, yellow, gold, green, black, bronze, white
	First, second, third
	High, high-horn, low, short
	Faint, vague, quiet, muted, silent
	Wooden, oak metal, metallic, iron, steel, straw
	Horizontal, vertical, rotating, spinning
	Blunted, edgeless, sharp, serrated
	Desperate, frantic, last-gasp
	Rowdy, noisy, loud, clamorous, thundering, booming, rumbling, resounding, reverberating
	Dramatic, spectacular, awesome
	Huge, large, massive, wide

Low, flat, off-centre

Slow, motionless, quick, fast, nimble

Outstretched

Odd, strange, unnatural, unusual

Verbs	**Arranged**, displayed, arrayed

Arranged, displayed, arrayed

Fluttered, flapped

Felt, sensed, detected

Spotted, saw, caught sight of, looked, watched

Blinked, narrowed, focused, stared, fixed, glanced, peered

Trickled, beaded, dripped

Heard, listened, sounded, warned, alerted

Hushed, silenced, murmured, groaned

Creaked, beat, drummed, clattered, whistled

Rose, rolled, surged, erupted

Neared, approached, advanced, entered, emerged

Signalled, indicated, motioned

Challenged, dared, defied

Hauled, yanked, pulled, shoved, pushed, dragged

Secured, barred, closed, descended, slid, opened, raised

Sat, poised, leaned back, rode, trotted, cantered, galloped

Nudged, squeezed, spurred, urged

Snorted, whinnied, pawed, reared

Clung, clutched, jerked, wrenched, wrestled

Gripped, loaded, lowered, pointed, aimed, lined up, raised, hooked, shot

Hung, dangled, spun, rotated

Waited, paused, halted, tensed, stiffened, braced

Crouched, huddled, slid

Edged, eased, inched, crept, crawled

Stepped, side-stepped, dodged, ducked, dived, threw, flattened

Spun, turned, twisted, whirled

Fell, tucked, rolled, somersaulted, landed

Scrambled, dashed, darted, ran, sprinted, plunged, flew

Reached for, drew, released

Lunged, launched, leapt, seized, caught, flung

Kicked, lashed out, looped, slammed, knocked, toppled

Hit, struck, nicked, slashed, jabbed, prodded, parried, blocked, fended off

Clashed, thudded, stabbed, buried, vibrated, jarred, exploded

Missed, avoided, evaded

PHRASES – NOUNS AND ADJECTIVES

- ★ From the end of the lists
- ★ From the pavilion
- ★ In the direction of the gallery
- ★ Towards the tree of shields
- ★ *Pennants and banners*
- ★ Famous knight
- ★ Flaming red dragon
- ★ Green and yellow background
- ★ A riot of colour
- ★ Vivid reds and golds and greens
- ★ Brightly coloured tabards of the pages
- ★ A vivid background of colour
- ★ Gleaming black harness
- ★ High-horn saddle
- ★ *Small, wooden shield*
- ★ Wooden ring
- ★ Plaited, straw circle
- ★ Bag of sand
- ★ Horizontal pole
- ★ Blunted lance
- ★ Black handle of a throwing knife
- ★ *Just above their heads*
- ★ Beneath his visor
- ★ *Straight out in front of him*
- ★ In a single movement
- ★ With his body flat to the roof
- ★ Over her outstretched foot
- ★ *In a moment*

* Without hesitation
* With one last, desperate effort
* Impossible to break free
* As quickly and quietly as he could
* *Only sign of life*
* Dim light in the stables
* *Cacophony of sound*
* Clink of spears
* Faint metallic slither of chain mail
* Trumpet blasts
* Drums and bugles, trumpets and cheers, shouts and groans
* On the third blast of the trumpet . . .
* *Rowdy cheer*
* An enormous cheer
* *Distinctive whistle of arrows*
* Sound of heavy feet
* Clatter of swords
* Clang of metal on metal
* Shower of sparks
* *Like a hammer blow*

PHRASES – VERBS

* As if time had stopped
* Time stood still
* As if everything was happening in slow motion
* As if the world was holding its breath
* *As he emerged from the pavilion . . .*
* As the white baton was thrown down . . .
* *As he neared the rampart . . .*
* As they spotted him . . .
* *Displayed the knight's arms*
* Fluttered in the early morning breeze
* *Had already spotted the shield*
* Hit it with his lance
* Challenged . . . to face him in a joust
* *Waited by the pavilion*
* Sat on his high-horn saddle like a statue
* Started to move forward
* Rode forward slowly
* Nudged his destrier forward
* Kicked his charger's flanks
* As his horse's stride lengthened . . .

- ★ Spurred his mount on
- ★ Broke into a canter
- ★ Urged his horse to a gallop in a thundering charge
- ★ Galloped towards
- ★ Sent clods of earth flying into the air
- ★ *Sensed the excitement of the crowd*
- ★ Began snorting and pawing at the ground
- ★ Reared up onto two legs
- ★ Front hooves pawed the air
- ★ *Jerked back on the reins*
- ★ Leaned back in the saddle
- ★ *Clung to his horse*
- ★ Fought to bring the horse under control
- ★ Wrestled with the reins
- ★ Tried to get to the end of the list without being unseated
- ★ *Pointed the horse at the quintain*
- ★ Gripped his lance like a vice
- ★ Lowered his lance down over the horse's neck
- ★ Kept his lance lined up with the target
- ★ Raised his shield slightly
- ★ *Dangled from the pole*
- ★ Rotated on the horizontal pole
- ★ *Rings had gradually decreased in size*
- ★ Like a wooden eye mocking him
- ★ *Hooked it with his lance*
- ★ Had hit the target off-centre
- ★ Nicked the outside of the smallest ring
- ★ *Met with a dramatic clash of lance and shields*
- ★ Felt the thud as his lance made contact with . . .
- ★ Felt his opponent's lance thud into his side
- ★ *Hurtled towards him*
- ★ Braced himself for the impact
- ★ As the . . . thudded into him . . .
- ★ Sent him crashing to the ground
- ★ Stabbed his side
- ★ *Stared down the length of the track*
- ★ Narrowed his eyes
- ★ Peered through the visor slit
- ★ Eyes fixed on the herald
- ★ Stared ahead
- ★ *Cast a glance over his shoulder*
- ★ Looked both ways to check the coast was clear
- ★ Peered warily over the edge of the battlements
- ★ Looked from side to side and over her shoulders

* Didn't look back
* *Sweat rolled down his forehead and into his eyes*
* Blinked and tried to focus
* *Couldn't see if there was anyone*
* Spotted two guards
* Saw the . . . hurtling towards him
* Turned to see . . .
* Caught sight of a glint of metal
* *Brought a hush over the crowd*
* Fell silent
* Sent the birds whirring into the sky
* Murmur rolled through the crowd of villagers
* Rose from the spectators
* Erupted from the battlements
* *Creaked with every movement*
* Drum began to beat
* Hooves drummed on the ground
* Echoed in the silence
* Thudded behind them
* Clash of blades sounded from above
* Horn sounded the alarm
* Heard the clink of spears
* *Until the bow was fully drawn . . .*
* Braced back, leaning away from the curve of the bow
* Pointed it into the sky
* Brought the bow down in a smooth arc
* Kept her eyes fixed to the tip
* Poised to release . . .
* When the tip passed down the target, she . . .
* *Knew he had moments before . . .*
* Until she was sure the guards had not heard her
* *Waited, motionless*
* Stopped dead in his tracks
* Stiffened as the sound of . . .
* *As he sat in the shadows . . .*
* Slipped further into the shadows
* Kept to the shadows
* *Waited a moment and peered round*
* Paused to listen for any unnatural sounds
* Held her breath, motionless
* Waited for his breathing to steady before . . .
* *Edged towards an embrasure*
* Eased herself over until she was on the battlements
* Hauled herself to the top

- Crept along the roof tiles
- Edged slowly towards the window
- Edged forward a few paces
- Stayed close to the walls
- Edged round the courtyard
- Paused . . . nothing stirred . . . edged towards the tower
- *Dropped to a crouch*
- Ducked down low
- Ducked into the shadows
- Dived behind the dais
- Threw herself flat
- Flattened herself against the stable wall
- Crouched down behind . . .
- Pulled her knees tightly up to her chest
- Made himself as small as possible
- *Rolled away*
- Rolled to the side
- Sidestepped around a corner
- *Crawled forward*
- Placed his hands and feet with extreme care
- Moved as silently as a cat
- Inched forward until he was close enough to . . .
- Inched away from . . .
- *Hurled himself out of the . . .*
- Grasped the rope he had left dangling outside
- Gripped the rope with his feet
- Slid faster and faster down the rope
- Hands burned as they tried to keep pace
- *As she fell, raw instinct took control*
- Tucked into a roll
- Turned the impact into a somersault
- Came up standing
- *When she signalled that someone was coming . . .*
- As the guards strode from the gatehouse . . .
- *Was on his feet quickly*
- Could not stay where she was any longer
- Scrambled to his feet and began to move
- Dashed to the doors
- Ran to the next corner
- Sprinted to the door, and dived inside
- Spun and dashed back to the stairs
- Plunged down three at a time
- Turned sharp left at the bottom
- Plunged into the maze of passages beneath the castle

- ⋆ Twisted and dodged as his pursuer advanced
- ⋆ *Flew down the corridor*
- ⋆ Barrelled past the door
- ⋆ Darted up the stairs
- ⋆ Raced towards the door
- ⋆ Dived inside the chamber
- ⋆ Ran, darting left and right
- ⋆ *Strained every muscle*
- ⋆ Hauled on the massive iron ring
- ⋆ Pulled the lever that operated the huge, iron bolts
- ⋆ Leaned against the wheel
- ⋆ Pushed as hard as they could
- ⋆ Began to turn slowly
- ⋆ *Dragged the huge, oak doors closed*
- ⋆ Secured the gates
- ⋆ Barred the doors
- ⋆ Started to descend
- ⋆ *Slid her dagger into the gap*
- ⋆ Eased the door open
- ⋆ Yanked at the handle
- ⋆ Wrenched the door open
- ⋆ Shoved the door open
- ⋆ Stood wide open
- ⋆ *Sky darkened above them as . . .*
- ⋆ Arrows rose over the wall
- ⋆ Thudded into the door
- ⋆ Vibrated in the wooden post
- ⋆ Plunged earthward in a deadly rain of wood and steel
- ⋆ Would have been buried near her heart if . . .
- ⋆ As a spear flew past his ear . . .
- ⋆ As a crossbow bolt exploded along the passage . . .
- ⋆ *Rubbed dirt into his sword so the glint would not betray him*
- ⋆ Struggled to get her dagger out of its sheath as she ran
- ⋆ Reached for his sword
- ⋆ Reached for the secret dagger
- ⋆ Kept strapped to his arm
- ⋆ Released the blade from its scabbard with a single movement
- ⋆ Drew the sword from her belt
- ⋆ *Held his sword out in front of him*
- ⋆ Clutched their weapons, staring ahead, waiting
- ⋆ *Lunged at her*
- ⋆ Seized him from behind
- ⋆ *Lashed out with her feet*
- ⋆ Took his knees out from under him

- ⋆ Caught the sentry in the stomach
- ⋆ Flung herself at him
- ⋆ Launched herself from the shadows directly at his feet
- ⋆ Leapt onto his back
- ⋆ Fell backwards and took the attacker by surprise
- ⋆ Kicked him in the ribs
- ⋆ Looped her arms over his head
- ⋆ Slammed as hard as she could into his shoulder
- ⋆ Sent him sprawling into the dirt
- ⋆ Knocked him off balance before he could loose his bolt
- ⋆ *Stepped nimbly aside*
- ⋆ Jerked to one side and then the other
- ⋆ Rolled to her feet quickly
- ⋆ *Thrust the arrow at him like a dagger*
- ⋆ As they slashed and struck . . .
- ⋆ Stood back to back, blades raised
- ⋆ Faced the soldiers who had surrounded them
- ⋆ Parried the first couple of blows
- ⋆ Sword arm circled in a blur
- ⋆ Grazed his neck and forced him to drop his sword
- ⋆ As the warrior slashed with his sword . . .
- ⋆ Fended off the first blow with her sword
- ⋆ Ducked underneath the blade
- ⋆ Parried, blocked, ducked and sidestepped
- ⋆ Found it impossible to penetrate his defence
- ⋆ Found it difficult to land a blow
- ⋆ *Sparks flew from their blades*
- ⋆ Clattered with a shower of sparks into . . .
- ⋆ Blade whistled as it sliced through the air
- ⋆ *Narrowly missed him*
- ⋆ Missed him by a hair's breadth
- ⋆ Ducked and the axe swung wide
- ⋆ Seemed almost to predict his thrusts before they came
- ⋆ Avoided blows that would have injured any other man
- ⋆ *Sliced at the knee joint of his opponent's armour*
- ⋆ Sent him toppling to the ground, his left leg useless
- ⋆ *As he doubled over . . .*
- ⋆ As the momentum of his attack carried him forward . . .
- ⋆ When he felt the hands closing around his neck . . .
- ⋆ *Jabbed their spears at him*
- ⋆ Prodded him forward at sword point
- ⋆ Kept him at a distance
- ⋆ Edged closer, tightening the circle
- ⋆ *Knew it was only moments before he was overwhelmed*

* Only had seconds to register . . .
* Descended to club him behind the ear
* Didn't have time to lift his shield
* Made his legs buckle
* Crashed to the ground in a tangle of arms and legs
* Fell senseless to the ground
* *Drew back the strings of their bows*
* Loaded a quarrel into the groove
* Leaned over the parapet
* Shot into the mass of soldiers below
* *When she looked up . . .*
* Looked up and saw . . .
* Caught a glimpse of . . .
* Silhouette crouched on the battlements
* Aimed directly at his head
* Quarrel hissed through the air
* Watched the bolt coming towards him
* *Made no attempt to riposte*
* Stayed crouched and braced behind his shield
* Drove back with every attack
* Grip on his shield started to weaken
* Jarred his arm
* Buried itself in her shield
* *Twisted in the grip of the captors*
* No matter how hard she writhed and kicked . . .
* *Listened with horror as . . .*
* Shattered the silence
* Could only hear the spinning of the quarrel
* Heard the echo of heavy footsteps behind him
* Warned her they were closing fast

SENTENCES

Alfred stared down the length of the track at the small wooden shield.

Gripping his lance like a vice, straight out in front of his body, Alfred kicked his charger's flanks, spurring it on. As its stride lengthened and they began to canter, he pointed the horse at the quintain, narrowing his eyes to keep his lance lined up with the target.

It was as if time had slowed. He felt the thud as his lance made contact with the shield and saw the bag of sand hurtling towards him, rotating wildly on the horizontal pole. Alfred braced himself for the impact as the bag thudded into him and sent him crashing to the ground. He had hit the target off-centre once again!

It felt as if the wooden circle dangling from the pole was like an eye mocking him. He still had not managed to hook it with his lance.

Each ring had decreased in size, and he had only managed to nick the outside of this smallest ring.

As Tom emerged, a rowdy cheer erupted from the battlements.

He rode forward slowly to the tree of shields, where the coloured shields were hung. He had already spotted it – the flaming red dragon on a green and yellow background.

Without hesitation, he rode straight to Sir William's shield, and hit it with his lance, challenging the famous knight to face him in a joust.

The lists were a riot of colour – the vivid reds and golds and greens of the pennants and banners, displaying the knights' arms, as they fluttered in the early morning breeze.

The brightly coloured tabards of the pages provided a vivid background.

There was a cacophony of sound: drums and bugles, trumpets and shouts, cheers and groans.

Suddenly, from the end of the lists, the trumpet blasts brought a hush over the crowd and sent the birds whirring into the sky.

John waited by the pavilion. As a murmur rolled through the crowd of villagers seated in a large group off to his left, he nudged his destrier forward.

His horse, sensing the excitement of the crowd, began snorting and pawing at the ground, its gleaming black harness creaking with every movement.

John jerked back on the reins and leaned back. The horse reared up onto two legs, its front hooves pawing the air. An enormous cheer rose from the crowd as they spotted him.

Beneath his visor, the sweat was running down his forehead and into his eyes. Blinking, Tom tried to focus, and peer through the visor slit.

A drum began to beat and the crowd fell silent. Tom sat in his high-horn saddle like a statue, his blunted lance ready. On the third blast of the trumpet, Tom kicked the flanks of his horse and started to move forward.

He lowered his lance down over the horse's neck, raised his shield slightly and waited, motionless, his eyes fixed on the herald.

As the white baton was thrown down, he kicked the flanks of his horse and urged him to a gallop until they were in a thundering charge.

The hooves drummed on the ground, sending clods of earth flying into the air, until the riders met in a dramatic clash of lance and shields.

Tom felt his opponent's lance thud into his side like a hammer blow. It was all he could do to cling to the horse and make it to the end.

A searing pain stabbed his side as he fought to bring the horse under control and wrestled with the reins.

Ann braced back, leaning away from the curve of the bow until it was fully drawn and pointing into the sky. Slowly, she brought it down in a smooth arc, her eyes fixed to the tip, poised to release the moment the tip passed down the target.

The wall rose sheer above Kitty so she couldn't see if there was anyone on the battlements. She flung a grappling line over the top and, as silently as she could, hauled herself to the top.

As Rob neared the rampart, he spotted two guards. Thankfully, they had their backs to him. He knew he had moments before they turned, so as quickly and quietly as he could, he edged towards an embrasure and peered warily over the edge of the battlements.

Cautiously, she eased herself over until she was on the battlements, and dropped to a crouch, holding her breath, motionless until she was sure that the guards had not heard her.

As Kitty fell, raw instinct took control. She tucked into a roll, turned the impact into a somersault, and came up standing.

Robert hurled himself out of the window, and just managed to grasp the rope dangling outside. As the clash of blades sounded from above, he caught sight of a glint of metal. Gripping the rope with his feet, he started to slide faster and faster, his hands burning as they tried to keep pace.

As the horn sounded the alarm, they dashed to the doors, hauled on the massive iron ring and slowly dragged the huge, oak doors closed.

Straining every muscle, they pulled the lever that operated the huge, iron bolts to secure the gates. To the left of the gate, however, a small sally port stood wide open.

They knew they only had minutes to lower the portcullis. With one last, desperate effort, they leaned against the wheel and pushed as hard as they could. Eventually, the wheel began to turn and the portcullis started to descend.

He stopped dead in his tracks as he heard the clink of spears and the faint metallic slither of chain mail.

They stiffened as the sound of footsteps echoed in the silence. Someone was following them. There was a thud behind them and they turned to see the black handle of a throwing knife vibrating in the wooden post just above their heads.

They stared ahead, hands clutching their weapons, staring, waiting. They listened with horror as the distinctive whistle of arrows shattered the silence and the sky darkened above them. Arrows rose over the wall and plunged earthward in a deadly rain of wood and steel.

When Kitty raised her hand to signal someone was coming, the others immediately ducked down low.

As a spear flew past his ear, he flung himself down behind the battlements.

Rob ducked into the shadows as the guards strode from the gatehouse.

Quickly, throwing herself flat, she rolled to the side just as a crossbow bolt exploded along the passage and thudded into the door. If she hadn't dived, the shaft would have been buried somewhere near her heart.

Looking from side to side and over her shoulders, she quickly dived behind the dais.

He pulled his knees tightly up to his chest, making himself as small as possible.

Slipping further into the shadows, she flattened herself against the wall, and crouched down behind the horses.

He sat in the shadows, rubbing dirt into his sword so that its glint wouldn't betray him. Behind him, Rob heard the echo of heavy footsteps. He cast a glance over his shoulder. In a moment, he was on his feet, his sword out in front of him.

He waited for his breathing to steady before crawling forward. Keeping to the shadows and moving as silently as a cat, he inched forward until he was close enough to overhear their conversation.

Slowly, placing his hands and feet with extreme care, he inched away from the pocket of knights sitting around the table by the fire.

He ran to the next corner, waited a moment, and peered round.

She looked both ways to check that the coast was clear, slid her dagger into the gap, and eased the door open.

Creeping along the roof tiles, his body flat to the roof, Rob gripped the tiles and edged slowly towards the window.

Staying close to the walls, Katie edged round the courtyard, paused . . . nothing stirred . . . a dim light in the stables was the only sign of life. She edged further towards the tower . . . paused again to listen for any unnatural sounds, then sprinted to the door, and dived inside.

He heard steps behind him, and peered over his shoulder. In a moment, he was on his feet, sword drawn.

She spun, dashed back to the stairs and plunged down three at a time. The sound of heavy feet, the clatter of swords, warned her they were closing fast. She didn't look back, but turned sharply right at the bottom and plunged into the maze of passages beneath the castle.

He flew down the corridor, and shoved the door open.

He barrelled past the doors that guarded the entrance to the hall. As he ran, he struggled to get his dagger out of its sheath.

Darting up the stairs, he saw a door ahead and raced towards it. He yanked at the handle, wrenched the door open, and dived inside.

She scrambled to her feet. Began to move. Time had run out. She could not stay where she was any longer.

Suddenly, he was out in the open, tearing across the courtyard, exploding out through the gate.

He ran, darting left and right, twisting and dodging, as his pursuer advanced again.

She reached for her sword and, with a single movement, released the blade from its scabbard.

Very quietly, he reached for the secret dagger he always kept strapped to his arm.

As quietly as she could, she drew the sword from her belt and edged forward a few paces, keeping to the shadows.

Kitty lashed out with her feet to take his knees out from under him.

He lashed out with his foot, catching the sentry in the stomach. As he doubled over, Rob leapt onto his back and looped his arms over his head.

The guard lunged at Kitty. She parried the blow and stepped aside, sending him sprawling into the dirt as the momentum of his attack carried him forward over her outstretched foot.

Someone seized Rob from behind, but he was ready, and when he felt the hands closing around his neck, he fell backwards and took the attacker by surprise.

Ann flung herself at him, slamming as hard as she could into his shoulder, desperate to knock him off balance before he could loose his bolt.

Katie launched herself from the shadows directly at his feet, and they crashed to the ground in a tangle of arms and legs. Quickly, she rolled to her feet, and kicked him in the ribs.

Stepping nimbly aside, she thrust the arrow at him like a dagger, grazing his neck, and forcing him to drop his sword.

They fell on each other, sparks flying from their blades as they slashed and struck.

John's sword arm circled in a blur, the blade whistling as it sliced through the air.

As the warrior slashed with his sword, he ducked underneath the blade. It missed him by a hair's breadth. Using his own weapon, he sliced at the knee joint of his opponent's armour, sending him toppling to the ground, his left leg useless.

He found it impossible to penetrate John's defence, to land a blow. John parried, blocked, dodged and sidestepped, seeming almost to predict his thrusts before they came, and avoiding blows that would have injured any other man.

They reloaded, drawing back the strings, loading a quarrel into the groove, leaning over the parapet and shooting into the soldiers below.

John made no attempt to riposte, staying crouched and braced behind his shield. He was driven back with every attack. Until now his defence was holding, but his grip on his shield was starting to weaken.

He parried the first couple of blows, but the shock that jarred his arm nearly made him buckle.

As she fended off the first blow with her sword, there was the sound of heavy boots rushing up behind her.

He ducked and the axe swung wide, clattering with a shower of sparks into the stone of the wall behind him.

He saw a movement out of the corner of his eye, but Nigel didn't have time to lift his shield. He only had seconds to register the shadow of the raised weapon before it descended to club him behind the ear and he fell senseless to the ground.

An arrow buried itself in Ann's shield, and when she looked up she caught a brief glimpse of a silhouette crouched on the battlements.

Will looked up and saw a crossbow aimed directly at his head, the quarrel hissing through the air. Time stood still. It was as if the world was holding its breath. Only the spinning of the quarrel broke the silence.

It was as if everything was happening in slow motion as he watched the bolt coming towards him.

Every time he moved, the soldiers jabbed their spears at him, keeping him at a distance. Gradually, they were edging closer, tightening the circle, and he knew that it was only moments before he was overwhelmed.

She jerked to one side and then the other, trying to slip past, but there was always another guard to block her path.

They stood back to back, blades raised, as they faced the soldiers who had surrounded them.

They prodded him forward at sword point.

Katie twisted in the grip of the captors, but with so many soldiers holding her, it was impossible to break free, no matter how hard she writhed and kicked.

SECTION 3 – REACTION

WORDS	
Nouns	**Castle**, battlements, portcullis, walls, gates, arrow slits
	Crowds
	Presence, movement, direction
	Footsteps, chain mail
	Dangers, secrets, trap, attack, escape, retreat
	Lights, glint, night, darkness
	Dread, foreboding, unease, panic, fear
	Hope, determination, anger, fury
	Muscles, nerves, senses, pulse, adrenalin
	Rush, flash, surge, explosion
	Effort, strain, action, strength
	Body, back, spine, stomach, neck, hackles, forehead, nose, eyes, mouth, breath
	Pace, walk, sprint
Similes/ Metaphors	*A fist of unease; red mist of fury; like a fish hooked on a line; spread like prickly heat; like he'd swallowed a fiery breath; as if he'd been injected with a shot of adrenalin*
Adjectives	**Grey**, black, dark, gloomy
	Eerie, sinister, menacing, evil
	Steel, metal
	Tell-tale, unmistakable
	Alert, ready
	Desperate, frantic, last-ditch
	Cold, hard, harsh, severe
	Wide, staring, narrowed
	Sudden, unexpected
	Painful, searing
Verbs	**Approached**, neared, entered
	Darkened, plunged

Lowered, barred, secured, locked

Watched, observed, followed

Trapped, snared, cornered

Felt, sensed, thought

Acted, reacted

Waited, moved, walked

Lost, evaded, merged, disappeared, escaped

Sharpened, enhanced

Quivered, quaked, shuddered

Flared, kindled, clenched, spread, rushed, surged

Collected, beaded, trickled, dripped

Clamped, dampened, suppressed, stifled

Ebbed, subsided

Dried, flooded, swallowed, sucked, held, breathed, sawed, rattled, rasped, let out, exhaled

Narrowed, squeezed, blinked, glued, fixed, scanned, searched, looked, flitted, darted, glanced, flickered, flicked

Startled, shocked, scared, paralysed

Kept, maintained

Quickened, ran, raced, sprinted

Slid, released, gripped, tightened

PHRASES – NOUNS AND ADJECTIVES

- ★ *Some kind of eerie presence in the castle*
- ★ Inside a world full of dangers and dark secrets
- ★ Something evil
- ★ Like a menacing predator
- ★ *From any direction*
- ★ At any moment
- ★ For several nights
- ★ *Slightest bit out of the ordinary*
- ★ Too quiet
- ★ Sound of footsteps
- ★ Clatter of steel
- ★ Slither of chain mail

- ⋆ Tell-tale glint of metal
- ⋆ *Every muscle in her body*
- ⋆ Every nerve and muscle in his body
- ⋆ Constantly alert
- ⋆ On high alert
- ⋆ A rush of nerves
- ⋆ A surge of adrenalin
- ⋆ An explosion of adrenalin
- ⋆ *A quivering dread*
- ⋆ With a sudden feeling of dread . . .
- ⋆ Flash of foreboding
- ⋆ A fist of unease
- ⋆ *Fear of what was to come*
- ⋆ A presence she could not see
- ⋆ Pulse in his fingertips
- ⋆ *A desperate hope*
- ⋆ *A red mist of fury*
- ⋆ A cold, hard anger
- ⋆ *Wide eyes*
- ⋆ Narrowed eyes
- ⋆ Alert to anything that might be out of the ordinary
- ⋆ *Sudden, searing pain*
- ⋆ No time to think
- ⋆ No time to do anything but react
- ⋆ Ready for whatever came at him next

PHRASES – VERBS

- ⋆ *As he waited for the white baton to be thrown down . . .*
- ⋆ As soon as he had entered the castle . . .
- ⋆ As he walked through the gates . . .
- ⋆ As night approached . . .
- ⋆ As the lights went out one by one . . .
- ⋆ Plunged into darkness
- ⋆ Portcullis was lowered and the gates were barred
- ⋆ Felt that the castle had trapped her
- ⋆ Could almost feel the crossbows aimed at his back
- ⋆ *Didn't feel right*
- ⋆ Not sure what he expected but . . .
- ⋆ Sure he was walking into a trap
- ⋆ Waiting for its next victim
- ⋆ *Watching his every movement*
- ⋆ If they glanced in her direction

- ★ If she was spotted in the castle
- ★ *Sensed something behind her*
- ★ Sensed it reaching out to her
- ★ Sensed they were waiting, expecting her
- ★ Drawing her in like a fish hooked on a line
- ★ A presence she could not see
- ★ Knew it was there, lurking behind the castle walls
- ★ *Knew what would happen if . . .*
- ★ Knew she had to get away
- ★ Had to lose herself in the crowds
- ★ *Sharpened his senses*
- ★ Made him alive to every detail
- ★ Going to be the fight of his life
- ★ Couldn't dampen the dread of . . .
- ★ Quivered with the strain of . . .
- ★ *Rushed through him*
- ★ Surged through his body
- ★ Marked the passing of the seconds
- ★ Threatened to paralyse him
- ★ *Had collected on his forehead*
- ★ Trickled down the side of his nose
- ★ *Sent a shiver down his spine*
- ★ Made his hackles rise
- ★ Walked with his hackles up
- ★ Clenched in the pit of his stomach
- ★ Spread through his body like prickly heat
- ★ *Tried to clamp down the fear*
- ★ Tried to swallow his fear
- ★ Fought an underlying sense of panic
- ★ Even though his heart was pounding . . .
- ★ Knew he had to remain calm
- ★ Could not afford to make any mistakes
- ★ *Scared into action*
- ★ Could feel the fear ebbing away
- ★ Panic gradually subsided
- ★ *Could feel the strength surging through him*
- ★ Started to take root
- ★ Flared up inside him
- ★ As if someone had injected a shot of adrenalin
- ★ Kindled inside him like he'd swallowed a fiery breath
- ★ *Narrowed his eyes*
- ★ Eyes narrowed with determination
- ★ Fixed his gaze on the target
- ★ Strained to pierce the darkness

- ★ Watched his every move
- ★ Kept their eyes glued to the battlements
- ★ Searched for any sign of movement
- ★ Watched through the arrow slit
- ★ Observed the routes and routines of the guards
- ★ Flitted quickly upwards
- ★ Darted wildly from side to side
- ★ Glanced up
- ★ Glanced rapidly around
- ★ Flicked from the gates to the battlements
- ★ Moved constantly
- ★ Took in every detail
- ★ Looked desperately around for a means of retreat
- ★ Squeezed his eyes shut
- ★ Blinked rapidly
- ★ As he glanced back . . .
- ★ Couldn't see anything
- ★ *Mouth had gone dry*
- ★ Seemed to have flooded with saliva
- ★ Sucked in a startled breath
- ★ Could hear his own harsh breathing
- ★ Sawed in and out under his visor
- ★ Let out a long breath
- ★ Realised he had been holding his breath
- ★ Uttered a cry
- ★ *Quickened his pace*
- ★ Maintained a steady walk
- ★ Every instinct demanded he break into a desperate sprint
- ★ *Fingers tightened on his sword*
- ★ Hand slid to the hilt of her sword

SENTENCES

He was not sure what he expected, but it was too quiet. It just didn't feel right. He was sure he was walking into a trap.

The castle sent a shiver down his spine. It was like a menacing predator watching his every move, waiting for its next victim.

She knew she had to get away. The only way was to lose herself in the crowd when the gates opened.

Every muscle in her body tensed. She was constantly alert for the sound of footsteps, the slither of chain mail, the clatter of steel.

As a surge of adrenalin rushed through him, every nerve and muscle in his body was on high alert, ready for an attack from any direction.

She sensed something behind her and felt the hairs go up on the back of her neck.

Kitty was shaking with terror that at any moment they would glance in her direction. She knew what would happen if she was spotted in the castle.

Sweat had collected on his forehead and was trickling down the side of his nose into his eyes. He squeezed them shut and blinked rapidly.

As he glanced back, an explosion of adrenalin surged through his body and he quickened his pace.

He tried to clamp down the fear that threatened to paralyse him. This was going to be the fight of his life.

There was no time to think. No time to do anything, but react to whatever came at him next.

Even though his heart was pounding, he knew he had to remain calm. He could not afford to make any mistakes now.

She sensed something – some kind of eerie presence in the castle. She sensed it reaching out to her, drawing her in like a fish hooked on a line.

It was a quivering dread of a presence she could not see, but knew was there, lurking behind the castle walls.

As soon as he had entered the castle, he had been fighting an underlying sense of panic, and as night approached – the portcullis lowered and the gates barred – he felt the castle had trapped him inside a world full of dangers and dark secrets.

His back quivered with the strain of maintaining a steady walk when every instinct demanded that he break into a desperate sprint.

Something made his hackles rise and his fingers tightened on his sword.

The pulse in his fingertips marked the passing of seconds as he waited for the baton to be thrown down.

Suddenly, a rush of nerves spread through his body like prickly heat.

A flash of foreboding blackened his thoughts – he couldn't dampen the dread that as soon as he entered the castle something evil was going to enter his life.

He walked with his hackles up, alert to anything that might be the slightest bit out of the ordinary.

A fist of unease clenched in the pit of his stomach.

His instincts told him that if he could make it to the stables, he would be safe for a while.

Fear of what was to come sharpened his senses and made him alive to every detail.

As he walked through the gates, he could almost feel the crossbows aimed at his back.

A desperate hope flared up inside him.

Rob was suddenly scared into action as if someone had injected a shot of adrenalin into his legs.

He could feel the strength surging through him and the fear ebbing away.

She looked at him through a red mist of fury as her hand slid to the hilt of her sword.

Anger kindled inside him like he'd swallowed a fiery breath.

His fear was gradually subsiding, and in its place, a cold hard anger was starting to take root.

He narrowed his eyes and fixed his gaze on the target.

Her wide eyes strained to pierce the darkness, darting wildly from side to side.

She kept her narrowed eyes on him, watching his every move.

They kept their eyes glued to the battlements, searching for any sign of movement, any tell-tale glint of metal.

Glancing rapidly around, his eyes flicked from the gate to the battlements.

He risked a quick glance over his shoulder.

She glanced up. She couldn't see anything, but she sensed they were waiting. They were expecting her.

He watched through the arrow slit as the lights went out one by one and the castle was plunged into darkness.

For several nights, he observed the routes and routines of the guards.

He tried to swallow his fear, but his mouth seemed to have flooded with saliva.

He could hear his own harsh breathing sawing in and out under his visor.

He uttered a cry at the sudden, searing pain.

He sucked in a startled breath.

He let out a long breath he hadn't realised he was holding.

Part 2
Atmosphere and suspense

9

Storms

THE S/C-I-R STRUCTURE

A sheer rock face rose up to her right, and to her left, cliffs dropped away into a dark abyss. She glanced back one more time and then continued to climb into the unknown. **Even though she knew she had taken a step towards something sinister and final, there was no going back now.**

A cold, shivering wind blew on the back of her neck and ears like the touch of cold fingers. Suddenly, the whole world seemed unnaturally dark, as if it had been drained of all light before a terrible storm broke. She looked up to see a dark cloud that wasn't there moments before. Above her, a distant rumble like thunder grew louder, and the ground beneath her feet started to shake. Stones cracked and exploded, sending fragments in every direction. It was as if the mountain itself was being shaken. She couldn't stay upright and was thrown violently backwards, teetering precariously on the edge of the path. For a dreadful moment she was hanging in the air, **her legs flailing and her eyes widening in fear** as she lunged with her right hand. **Her heart raced** as she felt her hand beginning to slip, her frozen fingers scrabbling as her body swung perilously over the drop. Her shoulders were burning. She was losing her grip. Her fingers slid towards the edge.

WORDS

Nouns	**Menace**, force, fury
	Scene, image, vision, spectacle
	Thunder, lightning, sky, clouds, air, horizon, heavens, nature, elements
	Whirlwind, vortex, maelstrom

Bolt, fork, flash, flare, flicker, spears, arrows, blade, trails, guillotine blade

Clap, crash, crack, creak, groan, roar, screech, explosion

Voice, shouts, echo

Mountainside, mountain, hill, slope, cliff

Rock, gravel, mud, dirt

Forest, trees, trunks, branches, roots, leaves

Land, city, street, ground, building, castle, battlements, towers, courtyard, roof, windows, shutters, doors, room, hall

Water, sea, ocean, river, lake, current, waves, crests, foam

Ship, boat, raft

Rain, raindrops, showers, downpour, torrent

Wind, breeze, gust, gale, hurricane

Skin, neck, ears, legs, feet, stride, skull, hair, face, eyes, clothes, cloak, hood

Similes/ Metaphors

Like an exploding firework; like camera flashes; like the echo of a drum; a bulging blister of grey water; as big as telephone poles; grated together like broken teeth; like the touch of a cold finger; like a gust of icy wind; like an avalanche of cold; like being buffeted by a whirlwind; burst like waterfalls; misty haze like a veil; like an inky black finger; like some giant, invisible hand; like a huge fist pounding the sky; like wooden tentacles searching for prey; like a fist against the roof; tickled his ear like a feather; hunted him like a beast; tore with its invisible hands; like stabbing fingers; like they were being fired from a cannon; hissed and spat like a bonfire; like a writhing nest of vipers

Adjectives

Great, torn, jagged, forked

Bright, white, brilliant, dazzling, flickering, shimmering

Silver, grey, murky, misty, blurred, dark, black

Cold, icy, bitter, harsh

Huge, enormous, massive, gigantic

Heavy, dense, leaden

Thunderous, pulsing, powerful, dangerous, fierce, savage, vicious, ferocious, menacing, ominous, monstrous

Boiling, swirling, whirling, surging

Eerie, sinister, unnatural

High, sharp, piercing, ear-splitting

Sickening, dreadful, hideous

Verbs

Gathered, massed, grew, swelled

Darkened, blotted, shadowed

Lit, streaked, flooded, blinded, blurred, flickered, seared, illuminated, spattered, flecked

Clung, snaked, swallowed, blanketed, enveloped, encircled

Split, cut, ripped, forked, pierced

Blew, rose, blasted, gusted, strengthened

Hit, smashed, thudded, beat, pounded, hammered, shuddered, shook

Drifted, rushed, tore, dashed, wound, twisted, whirled, churned, writhed, swirled, flurried

Bent, wound, arched, shoved, pushed, tugged, pulled, yanked, dragged, forced, pressed, crushed, swept away

Tickled, prickled, tore, whipped, thrashed, buffeted

Struggled, staggered, trudged, gripped, clung

Whispered, whistled, sighed, moaned, hissed, spat, howled, screamed, shrieked, boomed, pulsed

Rumbled, rattled, creaked, groaned, grated, banged, thudded, echoed

Opened, parted, burst

Rained, poured

Foamed, churned, thundered, broke, crashed, slammed, battered, rocked, pitched, showered

PHRASES – NOUNS AND ADJECTIVES

* *At the mercy of . . .*
* An awesome spectacle
* From out of nowhere
* One moment . . . the next . . .
* At other times
* Within minutes
* *In front of him*

- Behind him
- Above them
- Directly overhead
- From the heavens
- Ahead and below them
- Ground around him
- Down the slope
- *Unnaturally dark sky*
- Murky black
- Boiling, black clouds
- Dark, storm clouds
- Funnel cloud
- Gigantic bank of dark cloud
- Layers of heavy, black clouds
- Fingers of swirling black cloud
- Swirling vortex of black and silver
- Maelstrom of cloud and rain
- Menacing whirl of grey and white
- Grey, ominous and threatening
- Powerful, dangerous and menacing
- Misty haze like a veil
- *Breath of wind*
- Cold breeze
- Bitter winds
- Cold, shivering wind
- Like the touch of cold fingers
- Surging wind
- Violent wind
- Ferocious wind
- Like an inky black finger
- Swirling cone of black vapour
- Like a gust of icy wind
- Icy shards
- Like some giant, invisible hand
- *Lightning bolt*
- Flash of lightning
- Savage crack of lightning
- A great flare of lightning
- A fork of lightning
- Flash of brilliant white lightning
- Flickering white light
- Trails of lightning
- Jagged spears of lightning
- Dazzling arrows of lightning

* Huge, guillotine blade of lightning
* Eerie light
* *Clap of thunder*
* Like an exploding firework
* Like the echo of a drum
* Thunderous echo
* *High branches*
* With a sharp crack
* Sickening creak
* Ear-splitting crash
* Sudden screech of anger
* *A trickle of water*
* Showers of heavy rain
* Wall of the storm
* *Far out at sea*
* Over the shore
* *A bulging blister of churning grey water*
* Dark, grey sea around them
* Menacing crests
* Huge wall of water
* Swirling current
* *Trunks as big as telephone poles*

PHRASES – VERBS

* *As if the world had been drained of all colour*
* Brought a feeling of dread and menace
* As darkness fell, the storm worsened
* As night approached, the wind strengthened
* *Looked up to see . . .*
* Wasn't there before
* *Dark clouds gathered*
* Massed above her
* Drifted across the sky
* Whirled up in strange clouds
* Darkened the air with boiling clouds of dust
* Cast long shadows down the mountainside
* Blotted out the sun
* Clung to the hill
* Blanketed the city
* Formed a misty, silver veil
* *Grew and swelled as if it was alive*
* Seemed to come from all directions at once

- ★ Did not just come from one direction
- ★ Gained power all the time
- ★ Grew to a thing of force and fury
- ★ Grew stronger by the minute
- ★ *Writhed and twisted*
- ★ Flurried and swirled around her
- ★ Like being buffeted by a whirlwind
- ★ Whirled around her
- ★ Hit like an avalanche of cold
- ★ *Whistled and sighed*
- ★ Shrieked towards them
- ★ Howled in the courtyard
- ★ Deepened its roar as it pounded against the doors
- ★ Rattled the bare branches of the shivering trees
- ★ Grated together like broken teeth
- ★ Banged wildly in the sudden gust of wind
- ★ Roared through the hall
- ★ Filled with the sound of its roar
- ★ Screamed through the trees
- ★ Howled over the castle
- ★ Shrieked through the courtyard
- ★ Heard the crack and groan of the falling tree
- ★ Echoed down the mountains
- ★ *Bent the trees*
- ★ Whipped and stabbed at the forest
- ★ Thrashed and writhed against the fierce gale
- ★ Arched from side to side
- ★ Wound itself round the ancient trunks
- ★ Tore at the bark
- ★ Made the branches writhe
- ★ Like wooden tentacles searching for prey
- ★ *Rushed towards the mountain*
- ★ Beat like a fist against the roof
- ★ Swirled like a hurricane from wall to wall, floor to ceiling
- ★ Flung itself at the battlements
- ★ Twisted round the towers
- ★ *Carried her voice away*
- ★ Stole their shouts
- ★ *Whispered across her skin*
- ★ Blew on the backs of their necks and ears
- ★ Tickled his ear like a feather
- ★ Made the skin on his neck prickle with foreboding
- ★ *As the wind shoved and tugged fiercely at him . . .*
- ★ Slowed his stride

- ✦ Pushed him along
- ✦ Crushed her to the rock
- ✦ Pressed her body close to the slope
- ✦ Clung on with all her might
- ✦ Forced him back inside the building
- ✦ Staggered back and forth, side to side
- ✦ Struggled to stay on his feet
- ✦ Hunted them like a beast
- ✦ Thrashed at his hair
- ✦ Tore at their cloaks with its invisible fingers
- ✦ Whipped his cloak
- ✦ Tugged at their hoods
- ✦ Whipped at his clothes, his hair, his face
- ✦ Felt the vicious whip of the wind
- ✦ Lashed their skin
- ✦ Stung their skin
- ✦ Battered his eyes shut
- ✦ Flew across his path
- ✦ Bent branches which slashed at his face
- ✦ Would have blinded him if he had not . . .
- ✦ Tore at her face like stabbing fingers
- ✦ As if they were deliberately trying to blind him
- ✦ Lashed their legs and faces with dirt and gravel
- ✦ *Blasted at the shutters*
- ✦ Smashed back and forth against the wall
- ✦ Gusted against the windows, against the doors
- ✦ Echoes bounced through the room
- ✦ *Rumbled in the distance*
- ✦ Rumbled closer and closer
- ✦ Followed almost immediately
- ✦ Crashed and howled overhead
- ✦ Boomed menacingly
- ✦ Struggled and howled in fits and starts
- ✦ Pulsed and rumbled ominously
- ✦ Shuddered with a crack of thunder
- ✦ Shook the house to its core
- ✦ Like a huge fist was pounding the sky
- ✦ Felt as if the ground beneath his feet was being ripped apart
- ✦ *Streaked across the horizon*
- ✦ Tore through the night sky
- ✦ Streaked through the streets like an exploding firework
- ✦ Forked through the huge, boiling clouds
- ✦ Spattered with lightning
- ✦ Pierced the sky

- ★ Torn apart by the jagged spears of lightning
- ★ Burst across the crest of the oncoming storm
- ★ *Lit up the whole scene*
- ★ Split the sky
- ★ Cut through the darkness like camera flashes
- ★ Flooded the land
- ★ Touched the roof of the cave
- ★ Lit up the sky above the mountain
- ★ Illuminated the sky with a stark, blue-whiteness
- ★ *Seared his vision*
- ★ Blinded him as it flickered in and out
- ★ *Clouds parted*
- ★ A hole opened in the clouds
- ★ Crashed together, boiling and shrieking
- ★ Began to swell and pour down in streams
- ★ Rushed through the trees
- ★ Burst like waterfalls from the mouth of the darkening sky
- ★ Shrieked through the forest
- ★ Began to pound his skull
- ★ As though the huge raindrops were fired from a cannon
- ★ Hissed and spat like a bonfire
- ★ Ran into his eyes and blurred his vision
- ★ Churned into a swirling, miniature hurricane
- ★ Snaked its way down the hill
- ★ Swallowed the mountain
- ★ Encircled the forest
- ★ *Trudged on through the wet and mud*
- ★ Soaked to the skin
- ★ Ran down his hair
- ★ Followed the line of his spine to his waist
- ★ *Trapped by the black blanket of sea and sky*
- ★ Looked as if the sea was boiling
- ★ Began to swirl and churn fiercely
- ★ Had become a surging torrent
- ★ As the lake boiled and churned . . .
- ★ Foamed as the waves dashed against the rocks
- ★ Churned the spray into foam
- ★ Rolled and rushed, churned and boiled
- ★ Hurled white crested waves at the shore
- ★ Thundered towards them from the sea
- ★ Swallowed trees and land, spread and swirled
- ★ *Battered the ship*
- ★ Broke against the sides of the boat
- ★ Rocked and pitched in the heavy swells

* Slammed head-on into the monstrous, black waves
* Showered them with icy seawater
* Twisted around them as if trapped by a writhing nest of vipers
* *Tore whole trees out of the ground*
* Exposed the enormous balls of the roots
* Swept away whole trees
* Hurtled past
* Reached out to grab the raft
* Dragged the raft along with them

SENTENCES

The whole world seemed unnaturally dark, as if it had been drained of all light before a terrible storm broke.

She looked up to see a dark cloud that wasn't there moments before.

Above the ridge, dark clouds were gathering, casting long shadows down the mountainside.

Layers of heavy black clouds clung to the hill and blanketed the city.

A gigantic bank of dark cloud was massing above her. It seemed to writhe and twist, growing and swelling as if it were alive.

Dark storm clouds sped over the waves to blot out the sun.

The clouds rushed towards the mountain, trailing veils of rain in their wake.

The storm was an awesome spectacle, but powerful, dangerous and menacing.

A hole opened in the clouds – a swirling vortex of black and silver.

Fingers of swirling black cloud came down from the sky to whip and stab at the forest.

The storm churned into a swirling, miniature hurricane, which blocked their way, pushed them back down the slope.

A funnel cloud snaked its way down the hill like an inky black finger.

The storm swallowed the hill in a swirling cone of black vapour.

The thunder struggled and howled in fits and starts, until it rumbled closer and closer, and crashed overhead.

Thunder boomed through the city, shaking it to its core, and streaking through the streets like an exploding firework.

The air shook as the loud, booming wind hammered at the trees, and thunder crashed and roared overhead.

Thunder rumbled in the distance, the sky continued to darken, and the wind blew harder, gusting against the walls, screaming through the ruins.

The branches, then the whole tree shuddered with a crack of thunder. Another explosion, but much bigger this time. It felt as if the ground beneath his feet was being ripped apart.

Lightning tore through the sky, blinding him as it flickered in and out.

An immense, dazzling, guillotine blade of lightning streaked across the night sky, illuminating it with a stark blue-whiteness and flooding the land.

Flickering white light burst across the crest of the oncoming storm.

White bursts of light, one after another, cut through the darkness like camera flashes.

Overhead, lightning ripped through one of the dark clouds, and the thunder crashed around them like a huge fist pounding the sky.

The cold breeze caught their cloaks, tugging at their hoods.

The breeze was cold, the sky grey, ominous and threatening, the misty haze like a veil drifting across the sky, bringing with it a feeling of dread and menace.

From out of nowhere, a violent wind began to blow from the sea.

The wind seemed to grow in strength and was soon screaming through the trees.

The bitter winds and harsh whispers rattled the bare branches of the trees, which grated together like broken teeth.

The tops of the trees were bending, arching from side to side, whistling and sighing as the wind wound itself around the ancient trunks, through the tangle of leaves, tearing at the bark.

The forest seemed to thrash and writhe against the fierce gale – creaking and groaning as the wind rushed through the trees, twisting branches, making them flail like the arms of monsters searching for prey.

The wind was ferocious, gaining power all the time, until it screamed over the castle and beat like a fist against the walls, flung itself against the battlements, howled into the courtyard, twisted round the towers, blasted the doors, smashing them back and forth against the wall with a thud, roared through the hall, swirling like a hurricane from wall to wall, floor to ceiling.

A cold, shivering wind blew on the backs of their necks and ears like the touch of cold fingers

A breath of wind ghosted past him, tickling his ear like a feather and making the skin at the back of his neck prickle with foreboding.

The wind carried her voice away unanswered into the dark night.

The wind swirled around her, then tugged at her, pushed her and crushed her to the rock: she pressed her body close to the slope and clung on with all her might.

The wind grew stronger, whirling up in strange clouds, flurrying and swirling, tugging at them, lashing their legs and faces with dirt and gravel.

The wind shoved against him as though some gigantic, invisible hand was forcing him back inside the building.

The wind started to howl, growing stronger by the minute, whipping at his clothes, his hair, his face. The bending branches tore into his face like stabbing fingers, as if they were deliberately trying to blind him.

The wind did not just come from one direction: one moment it was in front of him, slowing his stride, pushing him back. Within minutes, it was behind him, pushing him forward in another direction. At other times, it appeared to come from all directions at once to whirl around him.

The wind had grown to a thing of force and fury, darkening the air with billowing clouds of dust and tearing at their cloaks with its invisible fingers. Hunting them like a beast. They staggered back and forth, side to side, struggling to stay on their feet.

The sky darkened and showers of heavy rain poured from the heavens.

All he could see was a maelstrom of cloud and rain.

The rain battered the dry leaves that clung to the branches of the trees like dead hands.

The rain fell harder, forming a misty, silver veil; the castle a blurred shadow behind it.

They trudged on through the wet and mud, wretched in the cold and soaked to the skin. A trickle of water ran down from his hair and followed the line of his spine to his waist.

Rain began to pour down in streams, bursting like waterfalls from the mouth of the darkening sky.

Rain began to pound his skull as though the raindrops were being fired from a cannon.

The ground around him hissed and spat like a bonfire.

As fast as he wiped the rain from his eyes, water ran back into them again, blurring his vision.

They were at the mercy of the wind and waves. Ahead and below them it was dark. They were trapped by the black blanket of the deep, swirling sea and stormy sky.

As the wind rose, the light dimmed across the sky and the sea grew as dark as the sky; there was a rumbling as the waves grew, their menacing crests visible far out, churning the spray into foam.

As darkness fell, the storm worsened. It looked as if the sea was boiling. Then it began to swirl and churn fiercely, and foam as the waves dashed against the rocks.

The ship rocked and pitched in the heavy swells. It slammed head-on into the monstrous black waves. The foaming crests battered the ship, breaking against its sides and relentlessly showering them with icy seawater.

Lightning flashed across the surging water that rolled and rushed, churned and boiled, hurling white crested waves at the shore.

The river had become a surging torrent, a bulging blister of churning, grey water. It had torn whole trees out of the ground, and swept them away. Trunks as big as telephone poles hurtled past, their root-balls exposed, their branches reaching out to grab the raft and drag it along with them.

With a great flare of lightning, the sky rumbled and roared. A huge wall of water came thundering towards them from the sea, over the shore, swallowing trees, and land, spreading and swirling.

As the lake boiled and churned, the swirling currents twisted round them like a writhing nest of vipers.

Part 3
Creatures

10
Parts, size and shape

THE S/C-I-R STRUCTURE

It was as if the howling was coming from all directions at once. Then he realised – it was heading towards him. He could hear the scuttling of clawed feet as it moved closer to where he lay behind the rocks. It stopped metres from where he was crouched in the shadows. It sniffed the air. **The blood had frozen in his veins. He wanted to run. He couldn't move. Could only crouch lower to the ground. His legs were glued to the floor.**

The air trembled with every flap of its black, bat-like wings as it scanned the area. **He sensed something behind him; felt the hairs go up on the back of his neck.** He whirled round. **An icy claw of fear had gripped his chest.** He found himself looking into the beetle-black eyes and snarling face of a massive wolf. It stepped closer and then reared up on its hind legs.

It came at him in a blur of clashing claws and fangs. He ducked as its claws sliced the air in front of his face. Horror-struck, he watched, as its slavering jaws plunged towards his outstretched arm. For a brief second, he hesitated. **Then, his racing pulse sent a wave of adrenalin surging through his veins.** Pushing with his legs, he launched himself off the ground and was quickly on his feet again. Almost at once, its savage, serrated teeth snapped where his arm had been just seconds before.

He broke into a frantic, stumbling run, trying to put as much distance between himself and the creature as possible . . . to reach the safety of the trees.

He couldn't hear anything. Hadn't sensed any movement behind him. Quickly, he risked a glance over his shoulder. As he turned, it plunged out of the night sky, and sliced the air in front of his face. He started running again, trying to get out of sight . . . forcing himself to ignore the burning that was creeping up his legs.

When he reached the tree-line, he flung himself down behind a tree, trying to steady his breathing. And waited. **He knew he would have only a second in which to act. His eyes tracked from side to side, probing the edge of the forest.** All of a sudden, it emerged in the clearing. Seizing an arrow from his quiver, he fitted it and let it fly. The arrow flew towards its target in a shower of blue sparks, finding its mark in the centre of its forehead.

SECTION 1 – TYPE AND BODY PARTS

WORDS	
Nouns	**Body**, skeleton, torso, abdomen, waist, armour, shell
	Head, mane, tusks, horns, face, ears, eyes, tentacles
	Arms, hands, fingers, talons
	Legs, feet, toes, hooves, claws
	Wings, tail
Mammals	**Human**, man, hag, monkey, ape, gorilla
	Cat, tiger, lion, leopard, panther
	Dog, wolf, mastiff, greyhound, hyena, jackal, coyote, tapir, pig, hog, boar, ram, goat, bull
	Horse, donkey, deer, stag, camel
	Raccoon, weasel, badger, beaver, hedgehog, rabbit
	Rat, mouse, gerbil
	Bat
	Sea lion
Reptiles	**Crocodile**, alligator, lizard, iguana, gecko, snake, cobra, viper, serpent
	Tortoise, turtle
Birds	**Vulture**, buzzard, eagle, hawk, owl, gull, raven, rook
	Albatross, condor, swan, emu, ostrich, peacock, pelican, penguin
	Raptor
	Turkey, rooster, chicken
Insects	**Fly**, wasp, moth, dragonfly, bee, cockroach, beetle

Arachnids	**Spider**, scorpion
Fish	**Shark**, eel, barracuda, piranha
Molluscs	**Snail**, slug, octopus
Mythical	**Dragon**, griffin, sphinx, Pegasus, centaur, satyr, unicorn, minotaur, chimera, werewolf, Cerberus, Celtic war hound
	Basilisk, hydra
	Charybdis, Scylla, leviathan, sirens, mermaid
	Phoenix, thunderbird
	Dwarf, elf, genie, goblin, leprechaun, gorgon, harpy, giant, ogre, troll, cyclops, Grendel
	Demon, ghost, banshee, furies, kelpies, boggart, death spirit, tree spirit, water spirit
Similes/ Metaphors	*As white as snow; as tall as two men; as big as a skyscraper*
Adjectives:	
Colour	**Black**, charcoal, inky, blue, red, purple
	Grey, silver, pale, white, maggot-pale, dusty white
	Golden, yellow, bronze, red, crimson, scarlet, brown, copper
	Green, bright green, lime, slime green, poisonous green
	Gleaming, bright, shining, luminous, shimmering
Size	**Small**, tiny, minute, elfin, short, dwarf-like
	Large, enormous, gigantic, immense, colossal, massive, mammoth
Shape	**Narrow**, thin, slim, slender
	Wide, broad, stubby, stocky, squat
	Round, oblong, square, serpentine, stretched, flattened, humped, deformed, misshapen
	Double-headed, wingless, long-finned
Appearance/ Character	**Ugly**, vile, hideous, monstrous, repulsive, ghastly, grotesque
	Fierce, brutal, savage, violent, vicious, menacing, merciless, venomous, malicious, ferocious, fiendish, malevolent, frightening, terrifying, petrifying
	Sly, crafty, cunning
	Ancient, wrinkled, wizened

PHRASES – NOUNS AND ADJECTIVES

- Horned ogre
- Skeleton of a giant horse
- Half-human, half-hyena
- Part ape, part scorpion
- Back legs and tail of a lion
- Slime-green body of a lizard and head of a badger
- Head of a horse, ears of a wolf
- Sleek body of a sea lion with a dog-like face
- Wrinkled hag with bat-like wings
- A great hydra with nine serpent heads
- Cruel beak, wings and claws of a griffin
- Horse-shaped kelpies
- Part mastiff, part greyhound, part wolf
- A double-headed serpent with the body of a giant black widow spider
- Hideous, red creature with eight legs, the head of a fly and a snake for a tail
- Ferocious, rooster-like animal with tentacles
- Tiny, vicious goblin with a scarlet rat's tail
- Savage spirit like a rooster from behind, with the front of a hyena
- Terrifying, eight-legged monster with chicken feet and the tusk of a rhino
- Vicious spirit in the shape of a gerbil
- Large, flying beast with the wings of a giant bat, the body of an enormous, white stag and the legs of a raptor
- Something between an ancient hag and a gigantic chicken
- Enormous, silver, serpentine creature with bat-like wings and a long-finned tail
- Sleek, black body of a panther with the wings and head of an eagle
- A black leviathan – half-lizard, half-snake
- Spider-like creature with a fat, poisonous body
- Head of a stag, with a human face and unblinking eyes like an owl
- Huge creature like a lion with a black mane and a long, black whip-like tail, with a hooded cobra at the tip
- Deformed, dwarf-like creature with leathery wings and hooked claws
- A hideous, gleaming black, wingless moth with a huge, skull-like head and barbed legs
- Human from the waist down, clad in metal armour, with scaly dragon's legs
- Tiny, elfin body
- Minute goblin with a lizard's tail
- Huge, white, ghostly spider
- Enormous dragonfly with the wingspan of an albatross
- Lime-green bat as large as an eagle
- Snake as short and thick as his forearm

- Massive, purple snake, with long coils as thick as his body and twice his height
- Two-feet tall with a thin body and limbs
- Giant, three-headed Cerberus
- Shaggy monster the size of a bull
- About the size of a large dog
- Twice his height
- Hulking, black ape-like creature
- Spider the size of a cat
- Butterfly bigger than an owl
- Ten times the size of an eagle
- Well over fifteen feet tall with enormous shoulders
- As tall as two men
- As big as a skyscraper
- As high as a mountain
- Tall, thick and wider than a doorway
- Almost as tall as the trees
- Nearly as big as an eagle
- Almost as wide as it was tall
- Bulging muscles on its arms and chest
- Serpentine creature with eight, scuttling, cockroach legs
- A single spider-leg
- Bulbous, black abdomen
- Long and sleek
- Jointed body like an insect
- Bulging, spider-shaped body
- Misshapen body
- Like a humped rat with a snake-like tail
- A segmented monster with a single, trunk-like leg
- Hedgehog-like creature, with a long, flat shape like a crocodile

SENTENCES

It had the body of a lizard and the head of a badger, with thick, red feathers around its neck.

A vast midnight-blue raptor loomed above her.

Scuttling towards him was a hideous, black, wingless moth. It had a huge, skull-like head and a terrifying, demonic face.

The island was guarded by a fierce sea-monster with an enormous, humped, serpentine body and nine serpent heads, each with a cruel, barbed beak.

She was something between an ancient hag and a gigantic chicken.

The ogre was as big as a skyscraper, with muscles on its arms and chest that bulged as it brandished the enormous, wooden log clutched in its fist.

The vile creature was so terrifying that anyone who looked at it died instantly.

No one dared to go near the caves, which were guarded by vicious, female monsters with boar fangs, and hair of writhing, hissing snakes.

The three-legged bird had the huge wings of an albatross, the claws of an eagle and hog's tusks.

Scuttling towards him was a huge scorpion. The sun glinted on the sharp spikes sprouting from its ten legs and the air trembled with every flap of its black, bat-like wings and flick of its stinger-tipped tail.

As the lion-like creature stalked towards him, he spotted a hooded cobra arched over its back.

SECTION 2 – COVERING

WORDS	
Nouns	**Skin**, hide, feathers
	Spikes, spines, fins, quills, arrows
	Studs, horns, plates, lumps, armour
	Scales, tentacles, suckers, spots, warts
	Fur, hair, whiskers, mane, beard, tussocks, locks
	Plants, leaves, grass, vines, seaweed, barnacles
Similes/ Metaphors	***As slippery as polished leather**; as wrinkled as a prune; scales as soft as silk; smooth like fish scales; like a massive, moulting parrot; fins like thin tentacles; spines like wire*
Adjectives	**Hairy**, woolly, furry, white-furred, fleecy
	Bare, hairless
	Fleshless, loose-fitting
	Metallic, steely, leathery, scaly, feathery
	Slippery, wet, moist, clammy
	Rough, coarse, thorny
	Dry, soft, silky, smooth
	Long, thick, huge, enormous, trailing

Sharp, stiff, bony, pointed, stinger-tipped

Straight, triangular

Untidy, moulting, wild, matted, tangled, torn

Living, bristling, squirming, flicking, hissing

Venomous, poisonous

Verbs   **Covered**, grew, clung

Hung, drooped, trailed, flowed

Stuck up, jutted, protruded, sprouted

Wrinkled, polished, glistened, gleamed, glinted

Oozed, bulged

PHRASES – NOUNS AND ADJECTIVES

- Bronze-skinned
- Pale, white skin
- Bright, poisonous green skin
- *Ill-fitting skin*
- Hard, leathery skin
- Thick hide of leathery skin
- Dirty, tangled hide
- *Bare skin around its face and neck*
- Practically hairless
- Skin was black and hairless
- *Skin as slippery as polished leather*
- As wrinkled as a prune
- A wrinkled hag
- *Furry body*
- White-furred wolf
- Fur as white as snow
- Yellowy fur
- Furry, brown creature with a single crimson stripe across its face
- *Dark, hairy body*
- Short, dark ruffs on its neck
- Long, black, matted hair
- Locks of copper hair
- Coarse, red hair
- Long, sea-green hair
- Thick tussocks of hair
- Hair of living, venomous snakes

- *Black, tangled lion's mane*
- Strange, feathery mane along its back
- *Billy-goat beard*
- Beard like a dragon
- Hairy whiskers
- Mane and beard like a bison
- *Scaly body*
- Snake scales
- Scaly, clammy skin
- Slippery scales
- Dry, red, scaly skin
- Reptilian scales
- Glowing, blue scales
- Red and white striped scales
- Smooth like fish scales
- Scales as soft as silk
- *Bird feathers*
- Feathers the colour of copper
- Gleaming feathers of scarlet and gold
- Mane of thick, black feathers
- Scarlet breast feathers
- Trailing black tail feathers
- Ring of crimson feathers around its neck
- Like a massive, moulting parrot
- Bright plumage, shimmering greens, reds and blues
- *Spikes along its back*
- Stiff quill feathers
- Steely hackles
- Stiff, rod-like hair
- Bristling, thorny spines all over
- Spikes like wire along its spine
- Porcupine quills
- *Body armour with spikes on its shoulders*
- Bony crests
- Tough, armour-plated skin with pointed, bony plates
- Triangular plates round its neck
- Heavy, overlapping plates of bone on its shoulders and wings
- Enormous tortoise shell
- *Stinger-tipped tentacles*
- Rows of suckers
- Masses of fins like thin tentacles

PHRASES – VERBS

* Ran from its head to the tip of its tail
* Ran the length of its body
* Travelled up the ridges of its shoulders and wings
* Ringed its neck
* *Drooped in loose folds*
* Hung loosely on its skeletal body
* Clung to its fleshless skeleton
* *Flowed to her feet*
* Trailed out behind her
* *Stood up to form a row of sharp spikes*
* Stuck up along its spine
* Bristled along its back
* Sprouted from its body
* Jutted out of its back
* *Covered in inky, black fur*
* Covered in heavy scales
* Covered in sharp, metallic feathers
* Dressed only in leaves
* Hair and beard made from living grass and vines
* Covered in studs, spikes and horns
* Covered in sharp quills
* Studded with bony lumps
* Bulged with green spots that oozed a yellow liquid
* Glistened like wet leather
* Glinted red and gold
* Matted with burrs

SENTENCES

She was half-human, half-hyena, with long, wild green hair.

It had thick, red feathers around its neck.

Its hairy whiskers were long, purple and twitching.

The five-headed, monstrous beast was covered in bulging, green spots.

No one dared to go near the caves, which were guarded by vicious, female monsters with boar fangs and hair of writhing, hissing snakes.

The sun glinted on the sharp spikes sprouting from its ten legs.

Below the waist it was covered in black fur, and above, stinger-tipped tentacles hung from its body.

Grinning maliciously at him was an ugly little goblin with a sly face, and hard, leathery skin covered in warts.

Bristling, thorny spines ringed its neck.

Masses of fins like thin tentacles clung to its fleshless skeleton.

11
Head

Nouns

Head, skull, face, chin, jaw

Skin, flesh, folds, hood

Horns, tusks, antlers, spikes

Beak, bill, snout, nose, nostrils

Mouth, jaws, teeth, fangs, tongue

Whiskers, feelers, crests, antennae

Suckers, tentacles, blow-hole

Drops, gobbets, ropes, stream

Venom, poison, acid, slime, drool, spittle, poison sacs

Similes/ Metaphors

Bald head like a turnip; horn spiked upwards like a thrusting sword; crests like red trumpets; teeth like spikes on a trap; fangs like hypodermic needles; teeth like tombstones; curved beak as merciless as a dagger; sharp tusks like a wild boar; like steel arrowheads; as sharp as the edge of a blade; spiked upwards like a thrusting sword

Adjectives

Small, tiny, large, huge, massive, enormous, gigantic

Wide, broad, thin, slim, long, short

Rounded, pointed, twisted, curved, curling, spiralling, corkscrew

Oval, cone-shaped, wedge-shaped

Pale, yellow, golden, pink, red, scarlet, orange, slime green, black

Bald, knobbly, bony, scaly, rubbery, steel, metallic

Sharp-beaked, cruel-beaked, horned

Ape-like, bird-like, reptilian

Sharp, razor-sharp, scissor-like, needle-sharp, hooked, forked

Bulging, sagging, drooping, sprouting, thrusting

Writhing, twitching

Dripping, drooling, slobbering, snarling, slavering

Ugly, hideous, grotesque, monstrous

Nasty, cruel, evil, savage, vicious, demonic, malicious, menacing, merciless, intelligent

Venomous, poisonous, stinger-tipped

Verbs

Covered, stretched, grew, sprouted, thrust, spiked

Hung, drooped, curled, curved

Lined, rimmed

Tipped with, coated in

Opened, unhinged, revealed

Lengthened, elongated

Bared, snarled, dribbled, trickled, drooled, dripped, slobbered

Flicked, flickered, tasted

Shot, spurted, blasted

PHRASES – NOUNS AND ADJECTIVES

- ★ Small, horned head
- ★ Scaly head of a lizard
- ★ Enormous, wedge-shaped head
- ★ Twisted head like a corkscrew
- ★ Cruel-beaked bird's head
- ★ Large, knobbly, bald head
- ★ Narrow head and bulging skull
- ★ *Ape-like face with a beak*
- ★ Narrow, pointed face
- ★ Oval, bony face
- ★ Long, thin, snarling face
- ★ Small, grotesque face
- ★ Malicious, demonic face
- ★ Coldly intelligent face
- ★ *Deathly pale, scaly skin*

- ⋆ Huge folds of sagging skin
- ⋆ Hood of purple skin around its head
- ⋆ Hood of slime-green and red skin
- ⋆ Chunks of missing flesh
- ⋆ *Horn in the middle of its forehead*
- ⋆ Golden antlers like a stag
- ⋆ Great, curled horns
- ⋆ Sharp tusks like a wild boar
- ⋆ Two long corkscrew horns
- ⋆ *Sprouting, rubbery feelers*
- ⋆ Stinger-tipped tentacles
- ⋆ Huge, spiralling antennae
- ⋆ Gigantic, writhing feelers
- ⋆ Head crests like red trumpets
- ⋆ Venom-storing blow-hole on top of its head
- ⋆ *Monstrous, slobbering mouth*
- ⋆ Massive, pink, circular mouth
- ⋆ Cavernous, scaly mouth
- ⋆ Grotesque thick lips
- ⋆ *Long, black, forked tongue*
- ⋆ Black reptilian tongue
- ⋆ *Scissor-like jaws*
- ⋆ Razor-sharp fangs
- ⋆ Thin, needle-sharp teeth
- ⋆ Savage, needle teeth like spikes on a trap
- ⋆ Rows of pointed teeth
- ⋆ Fangs like hypodermic needles
- ⋆ Teeth like tombstones
- ⋆ Huge teeth like steel arrowheads
- ⋆ Pair of long, dripping fangs
- ⋆ Teeth the size of a dragon's claws
- ⋆ A dozen rows of teeth
- ⋆ *Eagle's beak*
- ⋆ Parrot-like beak
- ⋆ Needle-sharp, metallic beak
- ⋆ Hooked, golden beak
- ⋆ Huge, rounded beak
- ⋆ Cruel, steel-coloured beak
- ⋆ Massive horned bill
- ⋆ Curved beak as merciless as a dagger
- ⋆ As sharp as the edge of a blade
- ⋆ *Stream of venom*
- ⋆ Venomous slime
- ⋆ Gobbets of slime

- Scarlet poison sacs
- Ropes of yellow drool

PHRASES – VERBS

- Covered in black hair
- *Drooped from its face*
- Sprouted from its head
- Hung from its head
- Curved from its head like a dagger
- Spiked upwards like a thrusting sword
- *Unhinged its jaw*
- Dropped open as if it had been unhinged
- *Flickered constantly*
- Tasted the air in search of its prey
- Lolled from its mouth
- Flicked far out from its scaly mouth
- *Fangs curled beneath its chin*
- Opened its mouth to reveal . . .
- Rimmed with shark's teeth
- Yellow teeth elongated into fangs
- Tipped with a needle of iron
- Coated in spittle
- Trickled from its teeth
- Capable of biting a shark in two
- *Filled with drooping tentacles*
- Tipped with suckers
- Dripped slime
- Dripped with blood from its last kill
- *Fire blasted from its open jaws*

SENTENCES

Huge folds of sagging skin drooped from its long, snarling face.

Its scaly head was like that of a lizard and was surrounded by a hood of slime-green and red skin.

Its small, narrow head had a rounded beak like a turtle. Its face was coldly intelligent.

It was small and wrinkled, with a large, knobbly, bald head like a turnip.

It had an ape-like face with a beak. Some of its flesh was missing, as if it had been eaten away by acid.

There was a single, spiral horn in the middle of its forehead.

It had a cruel, metallic beak that curved from its head like a dagger, and dripped blood from its last kill.

Two large tusks thrust upwards through the dense fur covering its face.

Huge, spiralling antennae erupted from its head.

Rubbery feelers sprouted from its mouth.

Stinger-tipped tentacles hung from its enormous, wedge-shaped head.

Her jaw unhinged and her yellow teeth elongated into fangs.

Its jaw dropped open as if it had been unhinged. An impossibly long, black tongue was thrust out.

Its grotesque, thick lips were coated in spittle.

A black, reptilian tongue flicked far out from its scaly mouth.

Its forked tongue flickered constantly, tasting the air in search of its prey.

It opened its mouth to reveal thin, needle-sharp teeth.

Its massive, pink, circular mouth was rimmed with shark's teeth.

Savage needle teeth tore at Kitty's legs, like spikes on a trap.

Fangs curled beneath its chin and dribbled with blood from its last kill.

A dozen rows of teeth circled the cavernous mouth.

Its hooked fangs were the size of a dragon's claws.

Beneath the tentacles on its face were a pair of long, dripping fangs.

It had huge teeth like steel arrowheads that were capable of biting a shark in two.

Venomous slime drooled from its razor-sharp fangs.

A stream of venom shot into the air from the blow-hole on top of its head.

Gobbets of slime trickled from its teeth.

Scarlet poison sacs were just visible behind its rows of pointed teeth.

Ropes of yellow drool hung from its open, circular mouth.

Its tongue lolled from its mouth, spraying them with foul saliva.

Fire blasted out of its open jaws, bathing the forest in orange flames.

The fangs jutting from its jaws were nearly as thick as his fist, their points as sharp as a spear.

 **12**

Eyes

WORDS	
Nouns	**Pupils**, sockets, orbs, whites, slits, stalks
	Back, forehead, skull
	Look, stare, glare
	Hatred, anger, greed, malice
Similes/ Metaphors	*Like diamonds; like two, bright coins; like slivers of glass; single, round eye like a spotlight; like flickering sparks; as big as headlights; moved in and out like telescopes; burned like furnaces; flared like a cornered animal*
Adjectives	**Black**, beetle-black, raven-black, grey, green, emerald, yellow, golden, orange, amber, brassy, pink, red, fiery, bloodshot, blind
	Long, large, huge, thin, little, small, beady, slitted, lidless
	Raised, bulging, goggling
	Bright, vivid, angry, fierce, glowing, gleaming, burning, blazing, flaming, ferocious
	Cold, dead, evil, cruel, dangerous, intelligent
	Unblinking, staring, piercing, malicious
Verbs	**Lit**, cast, shone, burned, flared, blazed, gleamed, glinted, glowed, glittered
	Looked, watched, stared, glared, drilled, twitched, flickered, bulged

PHRASES – NOUNS AND ADJECTIVES

- ★ Beady, beetle-black eyes
- ★ Raven-black eyes
- ★ Thin, slitted, black pupils
- ★ *Eyes like bulging emerald balls*
- ★ Bright green eyes
- ★ *Single, bloodshot eye*
- ★ Pink orbs of its eyes
- ★ Glowing, red eyes
- ★ Piercing, red eyes
- ★ Blazing, bloodshot eyes
- ★ *Goggling, yellow eyes*
- ★ Two amber eyes
- ★ Amber-coloured, reptilian eyes
- ★ Bulging, orange eyes
- ★ Raised brassy eyes
- ★ *Blind eye sockets*
- ★ Eye sockets but no eyes
- ★ Clearly blind
- ★ Single eye like a spotlight
- ★ Middle of its forehead
- ★ On top of long, thin stalks
- ★ On rubbery, twitching eye-stalks
- ★ *Two raised little bat eyes*
- ★ Long slits
- ★ *Size of headlights*
- ★ Huge, cold eyes
- ★ *Unblinking eyes*
- ★ Cold, lidless stare
- ★ Malicious, staring eyes
- ★ Cold and calculating
- ★ Disturbingly intelligent
- ★ Flaming, red eyes
- ★ Full of hatred and anger
- ★ Bulging and fierce in its hideous face

PHRASES – VERBS

- ★ Dotted along its back
- ★ Bulged out of its skull
- ★ Looked in different directions
- ★ Cast wide beams of light

* ⋆ Burned like furnaces
* ⋆ Flared like a cornered animal
* ⋆ Flickered with a dangerous light
* ⋆ Burned with a cruel light
* ⋆ Glowed like flickering sparks in the dark
* ⋆ Glinted with greed
* ⋆ Gleamed maliciously
* ⋆ Glittered with intelligence
* ⋆ *Watched from the shadows*
* ⋆ Drilled into her

SENTENCES

Its beady, black eyes glinted with greed.

Its red eyes burned with a cruel light from its long, snarling face.

Goggling, yellow eyes glinted from rubbery, twitching eye-stalks.

It had a single, round orange eye in the middle of its forehead.

Its glowing, red eyes were bulging and fierce in its grotesque face.

Its eyes were the size of headlights and cast wide beams of light on the ground in front of it.

She closed her eyes to escape the cold, staring eyes that drilled into her from his sharp-beaked bird's head.

Above a curved beak as sharp as a blade, its bulging orange eyes burned like furnaces.

Its eyes were on top of long stalks, which twisted and writhed as they followed Kitty's every movement.

It had piercing, red eyes, which glowed like flickering sparks in the dark.

Its beetle-black eyes were bright with malice.

As she looked at its eye sockets, she realised that it was clearly blind.

Its eyes were on long horns like snail's eyes, and could move in and out like telescopes.

Its raven-black eyes looked disturbingly intelligent – cold and calculating.

Its reptilian eyes flickered with a dangerous light as it watched her from the shadows.

The thin, slitted black pupils of its amber-coloured, reptilian eyes regarded him with a cold and lidless stare.

13

Arms and legs

SECTION 1 – ARMS AND HANDS

WORDS	
Nouns	**Fingers**, knuckles, wrists, fingernails
	Suckers, claws, talons, tentacles, stumps
Similes/ Metaphors	*Like rippling octopus tentacles; long, hairy arms like a baboon; arms like stumps; claws as long and thick as a thumb; talons as long as a finger; as sharp as a dagger; arms as sharp as razor blades; as sharp as needles; hooked claws like coat hangers; wriggled like mindless maggots; extended like bony switchblades*
Adjectives	**Long**, short, skinny, fat, huge, giant
	Bird-like, webbed
	Woolly, brass, steel
	Sharp, sharp-clawed, curved, hooked
	Dead, lifeless, pale
	Deadly, menacing
Verbs	**Dangled**, dragged, scraped
	Spread, folded, extended, displayed, wriggled
	Fused, bound, merged
	Shot, flicked, whipped
	Sharpened, honed

PHRASES – NOUNS AND ADJECTIVES

- ★ On the end of her fingers
- ★ From the end of its tentacles
- ★ Each of its six fingers
- ★ *Long arms like rippling octopus tentacles*
- ★ Great, long, hairy arms like a baboon
- ★ Short arms like stumps
- ★ Small, useless stumps with webbed fingers
- ★ Short, skinny, woolly arms
- ★ Short, bird-like arms
- ★ *Webbed hands*
- ★ Sharp-clawed hands
- ★ Six fingers on each hand
- ★ Suckers on the ends of its hands
- ★ Lifeless hands
- ★ *Dead, white fingers*
- ★ Claws as long and thick as a thumb
- ★ Deadly, brass talons
- ★ Giant, steel claws
- ★ Razor talons
- ★ As sharp as razor blades
- ★ Points as sharp as needles
- ★ Huge, menacing claws as sharp as a dagger
- ★ Hooked claws like coat hangers
- ★ Long, deadly, eagle talons on its fingers

PHRASES – VERBS

- ★ Dragged along the ground
- ★ Folded, bird-like, under its shoulders
- ★ Dangled from its wrists
- ★ Extended like bony switchblades
- ★ Fused together to make a honed set of sharpened claws
- ★ Wriggled like mindless maggots
- ★ Scraped tracks in the earth
- ★ Displayed its claws
- ★ Shot out barely a hair's breadth from his face
- ★ Flipped out and whipped towards him

SENTENCES

Its arms were small, useless stumps with webbed fingers.

There were long, deadly, brass talons on the ends of her fingers.

Each of its six fingers had claws as sharp as razor blades.

The ends of its fingers were speared by hooked claws like coat hangers.

Its arms were long like a baboon, and as it walked, its knuckles grazed along the ground.

It had short arms that folded, bird-like, under its shoulders.

Its fingers and fingernails had fused together to make a honed set of sharpened claws.

Dead, white fingers wriggled like mindless maggots from the end of its octopus tentacles.

As its long arms dragged along the ground, its huge, menacing claws scraped tracks in the earth.

It opened its hand and displayed its claws, which had points as sharp as daggers.

Razor-sharp talons as long as his fingers shot out from its claws barely a hair's breadth from his face.

One of its tentacles suddenly flicked out and whipped along the ground towards him.

SECTION 2 – LEGS AND FEET

WORDS

Nouns	**Footprints**, foot, toes, paws
	Claws, talons, spurs, suction cups
	Mist, acid, venom, poison sacs, glands
	Goat, lion, horse, hippopotamus, octopus, vulture, chicken
Similes/ Metaphors	*Like tree trunks; claws the size of a butcher's knife; claws the size of a sword*
Adjectives	**Short**, long, tiny, small, large, giant
	Thick, thin, skinny
	Scaly, furry

Two-legged, four-toed, clawed, scythe-like

Sharp, jagged, barbed

Agile, powerful, clumsy

Scuttling

Verbs   **Faced**, pointed, extended

Acted as, ended with, tipped with, linked to

Crawled, shuffled, scuttled

Bared, revealed

Gushed, spouted

PHRASES – NOUNS AND ADJECTIVES

- Tree-trunk legs
- Thin, two-legged beast
- Legs like a horse
- Legs of a goat and eagle talons
- Six, short, thick legs like a hippopotamus
- Six, octopus-like legs
- Hind legs like tree trunks
- Front legs shorter than the hind legs
- Tiny front legs
- Short, skinny front legs
- Powerful front legs
- Powerful hind legs and a kangaroo tail
- Cushioned, furry paws
- Long, agile legs and four-toed feet
- Two, scaly legs
- A dozen, skittering legs
- *Spurs on its front legs*
- Lion paws and vulture claws
- Single large foot
- Giant, chicken feet
- Two, scaled chicken feet
- Large tortoise feet
- Seven clawed toes on each foot
- Claws the size of a sword
- Claws the size of a butcher's knife
- Suction cups on the tips of its toes
- Brown, poisonous mist

PHRASES – VERBS

- ⋆ Extended from a thick leg in the middle of its body
- ⋆ Feet faced backwards and forwards
- ⋆ *Used to crawl on all fours*
- ⋆ Used its front legs to . . .
- ⋆ Shuffled clumsily
- ⋆ Acted as a tripod
- ⋆ *Ended in sharp claws*
- ⋆ Ended in jagged claws
- ⋆ Linked to poison glands in its body
- ⋆ Tipped with vicious talons
- ⋆ Tipped with vulture claws
- ⋆ Gushed from the spurs
- ⋆ Bared its scythe-like claws

SENTENCES

The spurs on its front legs were linked to poison glands in its body.

A brown mist gushed from the spurs on its powerful front legs.

A single large foot extended from one thick leg in the middle of its body.

The giant shuffled clumsily on its tree-trunk legs and large tortoise feet.

It was a thin, two-legged beast, with seven clawed toes on each foot.

It had legs like a horse and its cushioned paws were tipped with vulture claws.

It had two, scaly legs and giant, chicken feet that ended in sharp claws.

Its hind legs were like huge tree trunks, but its front legs were short and skinny and only used when it crawled on all fours.

It had powerful hind legs and feet, which were tipped with vicious talons the size of a butcher's knife.

Its powerful hind legs and kangaroo tail acted as a tripod, as it stood motionless, watching them with its darting, red eyes.

Its feet could face backwards and forwards, so it was impossible to tell from its footprints which direction the creature had taken.

The vile creature fell to the floor, and using its tiny front legs, it crawled into the undergrowth.

It had a set of six octopus-like legs that made a dry, skittering sound as they moved.

14

Wings and tails

SECTION 1 – WINGS

WORDS

Nouns	**Bat**, beetle, ostrich, eagle, hawk
	Body, shoulder, withers, sides, flanks
Similes/ Metaphors	*Unfurled like sails*
Adjectives	**Short**, stubby, long, huge, giant, massive
	Shiny, golden, black, grey, shadowy
	Bat-like, leathery, scaly, spiny, razor-sharp
Verbs	**Grew**, burst, sprouted
	Arched, stretched, flapped, beat, fluttered
	Circled, dived, rushed

PHRASES – NOUNS AND ADJECTIVES

- ★ Wings like an ostrich
- ★ Golden, eagle wings
- ★ Two grey wings
- ★ Short, stubby wings
- ★ Two massive blue wings
- ★ Shadowy, bat-like wings
- ★ Huge, black, bat-like wings twice its length
- ★ Shiny, beetle wings
- ★ Huge, spiny wings

- Long, scaly wings
- Winged death spirits

PHRASES – VERBS

- Sprouted from its shoulders
- Sprouted from the horse's sides
- Burst from its withers
- *Folded its wings against its shoulders*
- Folded back along the length of its body
- Unfurled like sails
- *Tipped with a razor-sharp talon*
- *Circled above*
- Dived towards them
- Sent air rushing through the trees
- *Arched her back and stretched*
- Sprang from the neck of her cloak

SENTENCES

Long, scaly wings sprouted from its shoulders.

Winged, death spirits haunted the forest.

Huge, black, bat-like wings burst from its withers.

Wings of leathery skin stretched between its finger bones.

It circled above, folded its long, scaly wings flat against its shoulders and dived towards them.

The winged, death spirits sent the air rushing through the trees with every beat of their huge, bat-like wings.

Each wing was tipped with a razor-sharp talon.

Two massive blue wings sprouted from the horse's sides.

Its golden wings folded back along the length of its body.

She arched her back, stretched and two grey wings sprang from the neck of her cloak.

Bat-shaped wings twice its length unfurled like sails.

SECTION 2 – TAILS

Nouns	**Lion**, peacock, lemur, scorpion, snake
	Spear, club, oar, whip, rudder, corkscrew
	Tuft, stinger, spines, tail feathers
Similes/ Metaphors	*As long as a peacock's; long tail like a squashed pine cone; like a scorpion; thrust up like spears*
Adjectives	**Large**, thick, heavy, long, broad, flat
	Scaly, bony, barbed, spiked
	Stiff, rigid, whip-like
	Scarlet, fiery, golden, black
	Poisonous, venomous
Verbs	**Ended with**, tipped with, studded
	Dragged, swung, thumped
	Thrashed, tossed, whipped, swished, jerked, beat, lashed

PHRASES – NOUNS AND ADJECTIVES

- ★ Thick, heavy tail
- ★ Scaly, corkscrew tail
- ★ Barbed, oar-like tail
- ★ Broad, flat tail like a squashed pine cone
- ★ Long, stiff, rudder-like tail
- ★ Long, lemur-like tail
- ★ Enormous, whip-like tail
- ★ Thick, swishing tail
- ★ Long whipping tail of a black dragon
- ★ Steel-bladed tail
- ★ *Glittering, golden tail*
- ★ Gleaming black tail feathers
- ★ Scarlet and gold tail feathers
- ★ *As long as a peacock's*
- ★ Long tail with a spear at the end
- ★ *Club at the end of its tail*
- ★ With a hooded cobra on the tip
- ★ Poisonous tail stinger like a scorpion

PHRASES – VERBS

- ★ Thrust up like spears
- ★ Ended in a scorpion's sting
- ★ Tipped with four, tall, poisonous spines
- ★ Tipped with a razor-sharp talon
- ★ Studded along the length of its tail
- ★ *Dragged along the ground*
- ★ Thumped on the ground
- ★ Used its tail to swing through the trees
- ★ Thrashed the air, searching for its target

SENTENCES

Its thick, heavy tail dragged along behind it. The club at the end thumped on the ground with every step.

Its tail was broad and flat like a squashed pine cone. The spikes studded along its length made it a lethal weapon.

It hung from the branch by its long, lemur-like tail and swung towards them, baring its needle-sharp teeth.

Its four, poisonous spines were thrust upwards like spears and thrashed the air, searching for their target.

The huge lion had an enormous, whip-like tail with a hooded cobra on the tip.

15

Smell and sound

SECTION 1 – SMELL

WORDS

Nouns	**Smell**, stink, vapour, stench, odour
	Meat, flesh, water, plants, seaweed, smoke, acid, chlorine, sulphur, decay
Adjectives	**Foul**, strong, bitter, rotting, decaying, poisonous, pungent, putrefying
Verbs	**Smelt**, stank, reeked
	Rose, seeped, wafted, released, drifted
	Clung, surrounded, enveloped
	Choked, coughed, retched, vomited

PHRASES – NOUNS AND ADJECTIVES

- ★ Rotting flesh
- ★ Stench of decay
- ★ Foul-smelling vapour
- ★ Pungent odour of decay

PHRASES – VERBS

- ★ Stank of rotting meat
- ★ Reeked of foul water
- ★ Smelt of rotting plants and seaweed
- ★ Clung to it like a rotting cloak

* Reeked of chlorine
* Smelt of smoke and sulphur
* Surrounded by the stench of poisonous acid
* Polluted the air with each beat of its wings
* Gave off a pungent odour

SENTENCES

Its breath stank of rotting meat.

The dragon's breath smelt of smoke and sulphur.

It gave off a pungent odour of decay and rotting flesh.

A foul-smelling vapour polluted the air with each beat of its wings.

The stink of rotting meat and decay clung to the beast like a rotting cloak.

Its fur reeked of decaying plants and foul water from years spent in the swamps.

Its breath stank of rotting meat and the blood from its last kill dripped from its fangs.

She retched as the creature drew near and the stench of decay and rotting flesh wafted towards her.

She was surrounded by the stench of poisonous acid squirting from the spurs on its front legs.

Even though it was invisible, she knew the death spirit was near from the pungent odour of decay and rotting flesh that followed it.

SECTION 2 – SOUND

WORDS

Nouns **Silence,** hush, echo

Noise, hiss, whistle, murmur, moan

Cry, howl, yell, yelp, scream, screech, shriek

Cackle, gurgle, snicker, snort, laughter

Hoot, squawk, caw

Call, trumpet, roar, growl, bark

Wood, trees, bark, branches, twigs, leaves

Ground, slope

Movement, feet, footsteps, hooves, paws, claws, feelers, wings

Similes/ Metaphors	***Like dry leaves rustling in the autumn breeze****; as if a giant had broken a stone slab; like a whisper of silk; cold and pitiless as the fangs of the mountain peaks; like several snake tongues flicking the air: ugly, wet sounds like giant spit-balls*
Adjectives	**Low**, faint, muffled
	Slithering, skittering, clicking, scuttling, padding, lumbering
	Hissing, sibilant
	Throaty, rasping, gurgling, sucking, snickering
	Deathly, mournful, cruel, vile, demonic, gruesome
	Eerie, sinister, unearthly
	Loud, bleating, high-pitched, shrill, ear-splitting, piercing
	Thunderous, deafening
	Wild, feral, snarling, wolf-like, vicious, venomous, full-throated, blood-curdling
Verbs	**Clicked**, rustled, snapped, scraped, creaked, shuffled
	Landed, shook, vibrated
	Heard, sounded, wafted, drifted
	Tore, ripped, rushed, shattered, rent, blasted, pierced, slashed
	Filled, surrounded, enveloped, masked
	Rang, stung, echoed, answered
	Lingered, drew near, died

PHRASES – NOUNS AND ADJECTIVES

- From all directions at once
- From behind her
- From overhead
- Near his feet
- Down the slope
- In the grass behind them
- *At the same time*
- With every second that passed
- Unlike anything she had heard before
- *Skittering noise*
- Clicking sound
- Low murmur

- Vile gurgling
- Throaty gurgle
- Gruesome, gurgling whistle
- Hideous, guzzling noise
- Sinister sucking, snickering
- Slobbering, slurping, chewing
- *Hissing calls*
- Sibilant hiss
- Venomous, hissing noise
- Rasping of a rattlesnake
- Rasping, slithering sound
- *Loud, hooting call*
- Deathly moan
- Long, eerie cry
- Shrill, whistling sound
- Demonic cackle
- Piercing squawk
- Squawking crows
- *Snarling growl*
- Low, feral growling – half-warning, half-threat
- Feral howling
- Wolf-like snarls and howls
- Yelping and snapping jaws
- Snorts and growls and clashing of teeth
- Mournful howling of hunting wolves
- *Huge roar*
- Full-throated roar
- Blood-curdling growl
- Bellow of anger
- Trumpet roar
- *Bleating scream*
- Piercing scream
- Unearthly screech
- Thunderous cry
- High-pitched, human scream
- Ear-splitting shriek
- *Beating of wings*
- Flap of wings
- *Drumming of hooves*
- Scuttling of clawed feet
- Sound of padding paws on the hard earth
- Lumbering footsteps of a huge beast
- Deafening, cracking noise
- Explosion of shattering branches

* Striking thump on the ground
* *Feral and vicious*
* Dark, cruel and threatening

PHRASES – VERBS

* *As it clicked its feelers together*
* Came from the direction of . . .
* Felt a gust of movement from the left
* *At first, it sounded like . . .*
* Before he could see anything, he heard . . .
* Heard it, though he still couldn't see it
* *Gave her a minute's warning*
* Coming after her, gaining all the time
* Grew stronger and stronger
* Grew louder and louder
* *Vibrated through the ground*
* Landed all around them
* Rustled behind him
* *Ripped through the air*
* Blasted across the clearing
* Wafted across the water
* Echoed through the air
* Echoed through the night
* Echoed down the tunnel
* *Filled the cave*
* Enveloped him, surrounded by . . .
* Masked every other sound
* *Lingered, filling the air with . . .*
* Drifted away, leaving a tingling hush
* Died to an anxious murmur
* *Rang in his ears*
* Stung his ears
* Rushed past his ear
* *Pierced the silence*
* Shattered the silence
* Rent the air
* *Turned to see . . .*
* Made every hair on his body stand on end
* *Came from its mouth*
* Rose from somewhere deep in its throat
* *Snapped branches, crunched leaves*
* Scraped against the bark of a tree

* Broke a twig
* Shuffled through the leaves, moving closer
* Rustled through the woods
* *Rose to shrieks*
* Screeched and screeched and screeched
* *Answered by more . . . down the slope*

SENTENCES

The sound of its piercing squawk rung in his ears.

It threw back its head and let out a mournful howl.

A loud, hooting call echoed through the night.

A blood-curdling growl ripped through the air.

The silence was pierced by a high-pitched scream high in the trees.

Before he could see anything, he heard a scuttling of clawed feet.

The sound of beating of wings gave her a minute's warning before it rushed through the air and dived towards her.

The sound of lumbering footsteps grew louder and louder, vibrating through the ground as the creature gradually got closer and closer.

A blood-curdling shriek somewhere nearby shattered the silence and made every hair on his body stand on end.

She felt a gust of movement, heard a rasping, slithering sound, and then, to the left of where she lay crouched in the undergrowth, came a vile gurgling, a sinister sucking, snickering unlike anything she had heard before.

16
Habitat

Smell and Sound 135

WORDS

Nouns	**Castle**, church, graveyard, house, fireplace, boot, pipes, sewer, drains
	Hills, mountains, rocks, caves, tunnels, underground
	Swamp, creek, lake, river, pools, sea, ocean, seashell
	Forest, tree, trunk
Adjectives	**Dark**, damp, swampy
	Ruined, deserted, haunted
Verbs	**Lived**, lodged, inhabited, guarded

PHRASES – NOUNS AND ADJECTIVES

- ★ Hill-dwelling creature
- ★ Trunks of large trees
- ★ Dark caves and tunnels
- ★ Rock crevices
- ★ Ruined castles
- ★ Deserted graveyards
- ★ Swampy habitats
- ★ Deep pools
- ★ Rivers with dangerous currents
- ★ Enormous rock in the middle of the ocean

PHRASES - VERBS

- ★ Lived in the mountains
- ★ Lived in caves and tunnels

- Lived underground
- Guarded the treasures of the dead
- Inhabited ruined castles
- Came out of the water at night
- Lurked in swamps and creeks
- Stood in the middle of the ocean

SENTENCES

It stood in the middle of the ocean and, at a distance, appeared to be an enormous rock.

It hid in the rocks and only came out at night to search for prey.

It lived underground and tunnelled through the earth, uprooting trees in its path.

The lake was guarded by a huge, humped monster that stretched from shore to shore. Its humps looked like islands dotted across the water.

 **17**

Movement

WORDS	
Nouns	**Legs**, feet, footprints, steps, stride, movements
	Body, back, haunches, tail, wings, talons
	Fingers, claws
	Head, neck, feelers, snout, tongue
	Undergrowth, trees, treetops, water, waves, swamp, sky, air, mid-air
Similes/ Metaphors	***Like a scuttling lizard***; *cracked like thunder; like a crab with a hunched back; like a curtain of beating wings; like wolfhounds sniffing for prey; like a projectile; lightning speed*
Adjectives	**Front**, hind, rear
	Leathery, scaly
	Large, massive, powerful
	Pecking, shuffling, scuttling
	Angry, furious, venomous
Adverbs	**Slowly**, furtively, covertly
	Awkwardly, clumsily
	Quickly, rapidly, swiftly, sharply, deftly, powerfully
	Angrily, fiercely
	Menacingly, ominously
Verbs	**Shuffled**, dragged, loped, lumbered
	Slid, slithered, skimmed, twisted, writhed, turned
	Ran, galloped, scampered, streaked, darted

Climbed, shinned

Spread, unfurled, unfolded, furled, stretched, flapped, beat, fanned, rose, spiralled

Swooped, dived, plunged, hovered

Twitched, lowered, dipped, flattened

Jerked, swung, rammed

Tasted, sniffed, breathed

Flicked, flickered, waved

Crouched, hunkered

Reared, uncoiled

Pawed, gored, prowled, stalked

Slunk, stepped, inched, edged

PHRASES – NOUNS AND ADJECTIVES

* Whirl of leathery wings
* A flurry of wings
* Powerful, swanlike wings
* Magnificent winged horses
* Massive talons

PHRASES – VERBS

* Left no footprints
* Galloped without any sound
* Stalked at night amongst the silent trees
* *Dragged its clawed foot over the ground*
* Ran in pecking strides
* Shuffled forwards
* Loped out of the shadows
* Swayed as it walked in a zig-zag path
* Edged forward, swinging its head from side to side
* *Slid its scaly skin over the gravel*
* Twisted and writhed as it slithered across the courtyard
* Slipped beneath the surface of the water
* *Passed in a swirl of dust*
* Scampered down the path
* Streaked across the room
* Darted out from the undergrowth

- Slithered very quickly in both directions
- Turned at lightning speed
- Moved in silence like a projectile
- Moved faster than any of them could follow
- Shinned up the tree as if it was a staircase
- Skimmed over the waves
- Shot across the water
- *Beat at the air and rose in a spiral*
- Reared up, spread its wings
- Furled its wings against its back
- Snapped its wings close to its body
- Circled around them in a spiral
- Unfolded its wings, and shot back up into the sky
- Stretched out its wings to beat the air in a deadly rhythm
- Fanned its wings
- Spiralled up through the smoke and flames
- Swooped out of the treetops
- Dived at the tree directly above their heads
- Plunged like darts towards the treetops
- Swooped downwards in a heart-stopping dive
- Spiralled down to find a landing place
- Swooped to a halt in mid-air
- Paused to hover in mid-air, wings flapping
- *Jerked its head up*
- Rolled its head from side to side
- Swung its head to and fro
- Dipped its head from side to side
- Rammed its head into the entrance
- Flattened out its neck like a cobra
- *Twitched its feelers rapidly from side to side*
- Lowered its snout to sniff
- Like wolfhounds sniffing for prey
- Tasted the air with its tongue
- Sniffed the air, taking deep breaths, trying to locate the scent
- *Flicked its tail with a furious rattle*
- Flicked its tail with an angry twitch
- Whipped from side to side
- Whipped its tail behind it as it leapt out of the way
- Waved its clawed fingers in the air
- *Landed on its haunches*
- Hunkered down
- Dropped to all fours
- Dropped into a shallow crouch
- Crouched on its hind quarters

- *Rose up out of the swamp*
- Reared up behind him
- Reared up on its hind legs
- Uncoiled itself to its full height
- *Pawed the ground*
- Gored and pierced the shadows
- Prowled restlessly
- *Took a pace towards her*
- Slunk towards her
- Stepped closer and clawed at the air in front of him

SENTENCES

It moved towards them and then passed by in a swirl of dust.

It walked slowly, clumsily dragging its clawed foot over the ground.

It stretched out its leathery wings and beat the air in a deadly rhythm.

Swooping out of the treetops, it plunged like a dart, diving at the tree directly above their heads.

It swayed as it walked in a zig-zag path, swinging its head from side to side.

Faster than any of them could follow, it shinned up the tree like a silent projectile.

Suddenly, it tasted the air with its tongue, then dipped its head from side to side.

It landed on its haunches in the middle of the cave, swiping at the air with its clawed fingers.

It stepped closer and then reared up on its hind legs.

18
Weapons/attack

Kitty's legs were jerked from under her as she was lassoed by the silk thread from its mouth. It snaked around her legs and wound round and round, until her feet were locked together by the sticky ball at the end. Waving her arms wildly, she grasped for a hold as she was dragged towards the cave and the spider's web.

Sweat had collected on her forehead and was trickling down the side of her nose into her eyes. Frantically, she squeezed them shut, blinking rapidly to clear her vision. Sudden hope surged through her. As she turned her head, she had seen a glint of metal . . . to her left . . . within touching distance . . . her dagger!

His muscles were locked. The icy breath had fallen like a mist and frozen him to the spot. He was unable to move, unable to run. **His mouth frozen in a silent scream, his eyes wide with terror,** he stood motionless as the beast towered over him.

WORDS

Nouns	**Prey**, victim
	Gorgon, sirens, basilisk
	Breath, mist, fog, wind, thunder, lightning, electricity
	Stream, jet, plumes
	Slime, saliva, acid, liquid, venom, ichor, spit, poison, poison sacs
	Stare, grip, song, harp, sound, noise, tune
	Skin, flesh, bones, mouth, muzzle, jaws, teeth, fangs, bite, tentacles, stingers, tongue

Hand, fingers, knees, ankles, grip

Tail, legs, paws, clubs, spines, warts, talons, claws

Horn, tusks, beak

Flame, fire, smoke, nostrils

Spear, javelin, trident

Similes/ Metaphors	***Force as mighty as a gale***; *gusts of air like a tornado; like barbed spikes on a trap; like the tusks of a boar; claws as long and thick as thumbs; as sharp as an ice pick; swung its club like a huge bat; like steel bands; like a knife through butter; like water dropped on hot coals*
Adjectives	**Huge**, massive, thick, dense, long
	Icy, cold
	Sticky, slimy, rubbery
	Sharp, pillar-like, barbed, serrated, dagger-like
	Green, yellow, scarlet, orange, black, metal, steel
	Dripping, streaming, frothing
	Venomous, poisonous, toxic, acid-laced, stinging, sizzling, smoking
	Deadly, powerful, savage, lethal, fearsome
	High, shrill, piercing, hypnotic, enchanting
	Snapping, slavering, snarling, blood-stained
Verbs	**Breathed**, opened, spat, shot, sprayed, spurted, squirted, belched, blasted, melted
	Trapped, lured, lassoed, hooked
	Played, sang
	Hypnotised, wooed, enticed
	Stared, glared
	Froze, paralysed, wilted, killed
	Grabbed, seized, gripped, wrapped, clinched, tightened, squeezed, pulled, yanked
	Carried, raised, slashed, whipped, lashed, plunged, slammed, struck
	Bared, snapped, tore, sliced, pierced, shredded, crushed

Blinded

Hissed, snarled, growled, roared

PHRASES – NOUNS AND ADJECTIVES

- Icy breath like a cold mist
- Dense streams of grey fog
- Trail of sticky slime
- *Thunder hawk*
- Massive wings
- Force as mighty as a gale
- Deep rumble of giant wings
- Spidery, crackling lightning around it
- Sparking electricity along its skin
- *Poisonous saliva*
- Powerful stream of acid
- Streaming jet of liquid
- Acid-laced venom
- Stinging, black ichor
- Thick, frothing, green spit on its mouth
- Dripping, yellow venom on its fangs
- Deadly poison from the warts on its skin
- Venomous spines on its legs
- Scarlet mist of venom
- Scarlet and orange poison sacs behind its teeth
- *Snapping jaws*
- Slavering jaws
- Gnashing teeth
- Fearsome bite
- Blood-stained muzzle
- *Pillar-like teeth*
- Long, serrated teeth
- Savage teeth like barbed spikes on a trap
- Dagger-sharp metal teeth
- Teeth like the tusks of a boar
- Steel talons
- Black claws as long and thick as thumbs
- Pair of lobster claws
- Massive tusk
- *Club on the end of its tail*
- Steel-bladed tail
- Long snout like a vacuum hose
- *Jet of orange flame*

* Thick, red puff of smoke
* Smoking nostrils
* *Spear tip as sharp as an ice pick*
* Shrill, piercing, hypnotic singing
* Deadly, basilisk stare

PHRASES – VERBS

* Paralysed prey with its venomous spines
* Laid a trail of sticky slime to trap its prey
* Lassoed its victims with the silk thread from its mouth
* *Stare turned him to stone*
* Froze him to the spot
* Felt a slow paralysis of numbing cold
* Instant death if one looked into its eyes
* Gorgon glared at him with her deadly eyes
* Wilted beneath the basilisk stare
* *Played enchanting songs on its harp*
* Sang as they rose from the water
* Sang the same tune over and over until the ship was broken on the rocks
* *Hypnotised by the song*
* Wooed them to dive into the water
* Sirens enticed him to throw himself into the sea
* *Swept great gusts of air like a tornado down onto . . .*
* *Carried a massive club over his shoulder*
* Swung its club like a huge bat
* *Raised his javelin and thunder ripped through the sky*
* Clapped thunder from its wings and shot lightning from its eyes
* *Fire blasted out of its open jaw*
* Opened its mouth, and jetted out a stream of flame
* Breathed a river of white-hot fire
* Lashed them with red tongues of flame
* Blinded by the flash of light
* Shot bolt after bolt of flame as it pursued her
* Engulfed by a swirling wall of flames
* *Could shred her to pieces*
* Crushed the life out of its prey with its teeth
* Tore the flesh from its prey with savage teeth
* Snapped its needle-like teeth close to her cheek
* *Spat out a powerful stream of acid*
* Squirted a deadly poison
* Could melt bones with a single blast of its acid-laced venom
* Squirted brown acid from its eyes

- Venom glistened on the tip of its stinger
- *Wrapped itself around her ankles*
- Pulled her to her knees
- Tightened its grip
- Wound itself around his chest
- Squeezed the breath out of him
- Slammed into him and hurled him across the street
- *Slashed at his legs*
- Whipped out towards him
- Seized her ankle and yanked
- Lashed around his waist, dragging him closer to its gnashing teeth
- Wrapped around her body, dragging her down
- Wrapped around his arms like steel bands
- *Sliced the air in front of his face*
- Plunged out of the night sky to peck at his eyes
- Grabbed her in its front claws and vaulted in the air
- Slammed him against the slope
- *Jarred his bones*
- Pierced his side
- Slashed at their skin
- Cut into her side with its claws
- Raked down either side of his head
- Dug its pincers into her chest
- Ripped at him with furious swipes of their claws
- Caught him on the side of the face with her claw
- Gouged into the chain mail like a knife through butter
- Plunged its poisonous tail into him
- *Burnt through his skin*
- Spat jets of green poison that smoked on the ground
- Snorted plumes of steaming breath
- Turned the floor into a steaming crater of melted stone
- Hissed like water dropped on hot coals
- Released a lash of flame from deep in its throat
- *Struck with its front paws*
- Lashed down like a whip-stroke
- Slashed with blinding speed
- Grabbed her with its enormous beak
- Pinned her to the ground with one massive paw
- Grabbed him with one of its long, thin sinewy tentacles

SENTENCES

Poisonous saliva dripped from its savage jaws.

Its pillar-like teeth closed around the body and crushed the life out of it.

The warts on its skin split open and it squirted its deadly poison.

It blew up like a balloon and squirted brown acid from its eyes.

It tore the flesh from its prey with savage teeth like barbed spikes on a trap.

Venomous spines shot from its legs to paralyse its prey.

Women and children were lured into the lake by the enchanting songs it played on its harp.

Keeping his eyes fixed to the floor, he avoided her stare, knowing that it would turn him to stone.

Whipping its head around, it spat out a stream of acid, which sizzled as it hit the ground at his feet.

Bolt after bolt of white-hot flames shot out of its mouth until the forest was engulfed in a swirling wall of flames.

As it blasted fire out of its open jaws, thunder clapped from its wings and lightning shot from its eyes.

It plunged its poisonous tail into him, shooting acid-laced venom into his leg that sizzled as it burnt through his skin.

He could easily imagine the creature killing him with one swipe of its massive paw.

It slashed with blinding speed and pinned her to the ground with one massive paw.

With a whip-like stroke, it lashed down and caught him on the side of the face with its claw.

It lowered its curved bull's horn, pawed the ground and slammed into him, gouging his chain mail and sending him sprawling into the wall.

It bared its needle-sharp teeth. Then, in a lightning fast move, it lunged towards her and snapped them inches from her cheek.

Enormous front claws grabbed her and lifted her into the air.

It plunged out of the night sky, sliced the air in front of her face, grabbed her in its front claws and vaulted in the air.

With blinding speed, it lashed in a whip-stroke, and cut into her side with its claws.

19

Interaction with and reaction to the creature

As the rasping, slithering sound drew closer, **a shiver charged down her spine like an electric shock.** She ducked back into one of the other caves and stood there, behind a pillar, not daring to move.

He was crouched behind the wall. Hadn't moved a muscle for ten minutes. Waited – still did not move. Still there was no sign. **He was certain that they were somewhere nearby. His eyes darted from side to side, probing the shadows, searching for the slightest movement.** To his left . . . a flicker of movement. Then another, above him, to his right. Another and another, swarming towards him. **His heart almost stopped.** They were coming at him from all directions; their giant, wasps' heads swooping towards him. He started to run, not daring to look back, **the sound of his breathing roaring in his ears, as his racing pulse sent an explosion of adrenalin surging through his veins.**

SECTION 1 – INTERACTION

Nouns	**Silence**, darkness, shadows, light, moonlight
	Head, face, knees, haunches, back, stomach, belly, chest
	Mountain, rocks, boulders

Woodland, tree-line, trees, branches, trunk, logs, reeds, foliage, leaves, pine needles, shrub, bush, hedge, grass

Cave, tunnel, wall, pillar, column, tomb

Floor, ground, ditch, trench, hole

Sounds, noises

Adjectives

Thick, wide, low, hanging

Dark, shadowy, gloomy

Automatic, instinctive

Verbs

Dug, scooped out, covered, concealed, camouflaged

Heard, listened

Saw, glimpsed, watched, looked, stared, searched, glanced, peeped, peered, peeked

Lay, sat, waited, poised, leaned

Hid, merged, submerged, vanished, disappeared

Hugged, pressed, pinned, wedged, flattened

Lifted, raised, craned

Moved, inched, edged, eased, slunk, crept, crawled, slithered, rolled

Stopped, paused, slowed, walked, headed, followed, reached, retraced

Slid, slipped, stumbled, scrabbled, scrambled, scurried

Dipped, bowed, ducked, dropped, dived, crouched

Sank, lowered, shrank, sneaked, backed, retreated, moved back, stepped back

Hit, threw, flung, jerked

Crashed through, blundered, shoved, slashed at

Turned, spun, swung, twisted, whirled, swerved, whipped round, lunged, avoided, missed, evaded

Quickened, hurried, fled, darted, rushed, ran, dashed, sprinted, bolted, hurtled, tore across, piled through, plunged

Dodged, bobbed, weaved

Climbed, jumped, leaped, sprang, bounded, pounded, vaulted

PHRASES – NOUNS AND ADJECTIVES

- *Out of the corner of her eye*
- *Just a few paces away*
- Only a stone's throw away
- Alarmingly close to where . . .
- *Nearer by the second*
- Within minutes
- Seconds later
- *Out of nowhere*
- In front of him
- Ahead of him
- Behind him
- Out of sight
- Invisible from just a few metres away
- Still no sign
- With every step, he . . .
- *For a fraction of a second*
- Barely time to . . .
- Just in time
- *Almost at the top, almost safe*
- With a new sense of urgency
- In a last mad dash
- Slowly, noiselessly
- *Waterlogged trench*
- Trailing branches close to the ground
- Towards the trees about a hundred metres away
- Through the twists and turns of the tunnel

PHRASES – VERBS

- Closing in on her
- About to turn away when . . .
- Just getting back to his feet when . . .
- As they were about to leave the cover of the rocks . . .
- When he reached the corner . . .
- All he had a chance to notice was . . .
- As soon as he was out of sight . . .
- *Without even looking up* . . .
- Not sure where it would take her
- *Hid amongst* . . .
- Hid when she heard . . .
- Looked around for a place to hide

* Searched for a hiding place
* Backed away and set about finding somewhere to hide
* *Slipped into the shadows*
* Lay in the shadows under . . .
* Slunk back into the shadows
* Stuck to the shadows
* Shied away from . . .
* Retreated into the shadow behind . . .
* *Shrank back against the wall, glancing from side to side*
* Backed quietly away towards . . .
* Staggered back
* Scurried for cover behind . . .
* Stopped, spun around, and dropped onto his belly
* Turned, and melted back into . . .
* *Dipped his head*
* Dropped onto her knees
* Ducked and rolled underneath . . .
* Ducked back into one of the other caves and stood there
* Ducked down, seeking cover behind . . .
* Dived the last few feet into the shelter of . . .
* *Lowered herself to the ground*
* Sank to her hands and knees
* Dropped his back against the wall
* Sank down at the base of one of the trees
* Slid back against the . . . onto his haunches
* Ducked down behind the . . . so he couldn't be seen
* Crouched behind the rocks halfway up the slope
* Bent down lower and peered through . . .
* *Dropped flat*
* Went to ground
* Hit the dirt
* Flung herself down behind . . .
* Scrambled for cover behind . . .
* Threw himself to the floor
* Scattered, diving for cover in the undergrowth
* Darted behind . . .
* *Had frozen in mid-crawl*
* Poised on one knee and one muddy hand
* *Dug herself in deeply behind . . .*
* Covered herself with leaves and pine needles
* Climbed up the oak until she found a sturdy fork in the tree where she could stay undetected
* Dragged herself into the tangled bushes at the base of the trees
* Scooped out a hollow under the bushes

- *Waited in edgy silence*
- Waited without moving
- Hadn't moved a muscle for ten minutes
- Waited a few minutes longer
- Waited silently in the shadows until he was sure that . . .
- Waited, motionless, for what seemed like an eternity
- Jerked her head back into the shadows
- *Sat cross-legged on the floor in the shadows*
- All he could do was lie still, hugging the ground
- *Crept along the floor against the wall until she was . . .*
- Crawled underneath . . . so that she was hidden by . . .
- Crawled to the edge of the bushes and peered out
- Rolled to the ground, flattening himself against . . .
- Rolled into the high grass so that she was out of sight
- *Flattened himself against . . .*
- Wedged himself behind . . .
- Pressed her back against . . .
- Eased himself up behind . . .
- *Covered his head with his hands*
- Wrapped his arms round his head and ducked low
- *Peered over . . .*
- Sneaked a glance at . . .
- Glanced up and peered through . . .
- Leaned forward so that she could see around . . .
- Edged carefully along until he was able to peer out
- From where he was crouching he could see . . .
- Leaned back out as far as he dared to . . .
- *Listened for the sound of . . .*
- Listened intently
- *Sprang to their feet*
- Scrambled to her feet
- Launched himself up from the ground
- Hauled himself to his feet
- *Began backing away slowly*
- Scuttled back to the shadows
- Retraced his steps
- *Headed towards the nearest . . .*
- Turned sharp left
- Fled in different directions
- Stopped when he reached . . .
- Made his way down . . .
- Scurried along . . .
- *Knew he had to move quickly*
- Forced himself to move faster

- ★ Tried to gain as much ground as possible
- ★ Tried to put as much distance as possible between her and her assailants
- ★ *Quickened his pace*
- ★ Raced towards . . .
- ★ Darted back into . . .
- ★ Bolted up . . .
- ★ Broke into a run
- ★ Ran blindly on
- ★ Ran on until his lungs were bursting
- ★ Ran for his life
- ★ Began running towards . . .
- ★ Started running again, trying to get out of sight
- ★ Ran faster, pushing herself to the limit
- ★ Kept on running, arms pumping, her lungs burning
- ★ Pressed on, running when he could
- ★ Hurtled towards the shadows
- ★ Dashed the last few yards
- ★ Turned blindly to the right at the end
- ★ Swerved to the right, down another tunnel
- ★ *Darted and dodged through the trees*
- ★ Ran, bobbing and weaving across . . .
- ★ Weaved in and out of the bushes
- ★ Ran again, slashing through the branches, heading for the darkest part of the forest
- ★ Dodged left and right down the warren of passages
- ★ *Crashed through the undergrowth, stumbling as she ran*
- ★ Stumbled towards the tree she had spotted
- ★ Blundered and slipped
- ★ Fought his way through the undergrowth that grasped at his ankles as he passed
- ★ Stumbled on the rutted forest floor
- ★ Tripped over rocks and shattered pillars
- ★ Slid on the loose stones
- ★ Stumbled over a ledge and hit the ground
- ★ Stumbled on, almost falling on some tree roots
- ★ Landed on his belly, scrabbled up and carried on
- ★ Slipped and slid in the boggy marsh
- ★ *Recovered his balance and kept running*
- ★ Managed to keep his balance
- ★ *Hauled herself up, edged along*
- ★ Pulled herself up onto the next branch, then the next
- ★ Climbed higher and higher
- ★ Leaped the low stone wall
- ★ Vaulted roots

- ✴ Launched himself down the slope
- ✴ Dropped the last few metres
- ✴ Crashed down on the ground
- ✴ Knew that it was a long way to fall if he slipped

SENTENCES

She caught a flicker of movement. Looking up, she saw it standing at the top of the slope.

Out of the corner of her eye, she saw a hideous creature crawling out from behind the tomb. A giant, wasp's head was attached to its black, porcupine body, on the end of which was a poisonous tail stinger.

It was heading in his direction. He could hear the scuttling of clawed feet as it moved close to where he lay in the shadows.

It hovered close to his hiding place. He could hear its flapping wings. Any minute it would look down and spot him. He had to find somewhere else to hide . . . and quick.

She was unaware of his presence, skulking in the shadows behind the boulders. She didn't look in his direction. He could see the hissing snakes on her head flicking their tongues, tasting the air. If she had looked for more than a few seconds she would have seen him.

The huge scorpion stopped metres from where he was crouched. The sun glinted on the sharp spikes sprouting from its ten legs and the air trembled with every flap of its black, bat-like wings as it scanned the area. He could hear the flick of its stinger-tipped tail in the dust.

She slipped further into the shadows and flattened herself against the wall.

Lowering herself to the ground inside the ditch, she waited a few minutes longer, and then peered over the muddy lip.

Holding her breath, she waited, sitting down carefully, drawing her knees up against her chest so she couldn't be seen.

Quickly, he dived for cover. Wedging himself behind a pile of rocks, he froze – motionless as if carved from stone.

Rob scooped out a hollow under the bushes and covered himself with leaves and pine needles.

She was crouched behind the tree. Hadn't moved a muscle for ten minutes. Waited – still did not move. Still there was no sign. She peered through the hanging branches.

Cautiously, Kitty leaned forward so that she could see around the trunk of the tree.

They all dropped flat, going to ground, and with an automatic action rolled into the high grass so that they were out of sight.

They walked for another ten minutes, neither of them speaking, and then they saw it up ahead.

Whirling round, she found herself face-to-face with the ape. Huge folds of sagging skin flopped around its long, snarling face as it swung its head from side to side, sniffing the air.

It was closing in on her. She knew she had to move quickly. Swiftly, she retraced her steps through the twists and turns of the tunnel.

It was as if the hideous squawking was coming from all directions at once. He quickened his pace, but the ground was uneven and he stumbled, crashing to the ground.

Hauling herself up onto the ledge, Katie edged along to the rail and grasped it with both hands.

Whirling to the left, she just managed to evade it. She sprinted down the hill, not daring to glance back, just trying to gain as much ground as possible.

She stopped when she reached the narrow track. She had heard something . . . the snap of a twig. She hurtled back towards the trees . . . the safety of the shadows.

Almost at the top, almost safe . . . almost. He forced himself to move faster, but he also knew that it was a long way to fall if he slipped.

She scrambled to her feet, and began to move, not sure which way to go, only knowing that she couldn't stay where she was.

He darted and dodged through the trees. Blundering and slipping, he fought his way through the undergrowth, which was grasping at his ankles.

Bent over, she tried to get her breath, risking a glance over her shoulder. She started running again, trying to get out of sight . . . forcing herself to ignore the burning that was creeping up her legs.

Faster and faster she ran, pushing herself to the limit, running blindly on, trying to put as much distance as possible between her and the hideous creature.

With a new sense of urgency, they plunged deeper into the cave, letting its shadows swallow them.

He launched himself down the slope, sliding on the loose stones, but just managing to keep his balance and surging on.

He rose to his feet, and sprinted to the wall, dropping to his knees behind it.

Never once did she turn and look back . . . just kept on running, arms pumping, her lungs burning.

She was up and running again, slashing through the branches, heading for the darkest part of the forest.

SECTION 2 – REACTION

WORDS	
Nouns	**Fear**, dread, panic, terror, shock, horror
	Brain, senses, sensation, nerves, pins and needles, breathing
	Prayer, hope
	Sound, noise, whisper, murmur
	Body, spine, arm, ankle, chest, stomach, head, eyes, throat, windpipe, temples, nose, lips
Similes/ Metaphors	*Like an electric shock; like a coiled spring in the pit of her stomach; as if carved from stone*
Adjectives	**Tingling**, electric, coiled, alert
	Wide, still, frozen
	Horror-stricken
	Urgent, low, tight
Verbs	**Gripped**, snaked, squeezed, choked
	Surged, raced, charged, pounded, hammered, pumped, blasted
	Warned, dared, felt, thought, knew, wanted, prepared
	Swallowed, gulped, stifled, gasped, winced
	Clasped, clenched, gritted
	Looked, strained, blinked, glanced, peeped, peered, d a r t e d, watched, closed
	Shook, shivered, trembled
	Collected, gathered, dripped, trickled
	Stood, waited, remained, froze, paralysed

PHRASES – NOUNS AND ADJECTIVES

- ⭑ No more than a whisper from the shadows
- ⭑ *At any moment*
- ⭑ A few more seconds until . . .
- ⭑ *Every nerve in his body*
- ⭑ Tingling sixth sense
- ⭑ Like an electric shock
- ⭑ Like a coiled spring in the pit of her stomach
- ⭑ Pins and needles
- ⭑ Wide eyes
- ⭑ Horror-stricken expression
- ⭑ Gasping, ragged breath
- ⭑ *Certain it was somewhere nearby*

PHRASES – VERBS

- ⭑ Tried desperately to think of . . .
- ⭑ Thought of what would happen if it caught her
- ⭑ *Motionless, alert and ready to move quickly*
- ⭑ Motionless as if carved from stone
- ⭑ *Prickled painfully in his ankle*
- ⭑ *Surged through her*
- ⭑ Enveloped her
- ⭑ Warned him not to make a sound
- ⭑ Wanted to get up and run
- ⭑ Knew she couldn't move
- ⭑ Didn't dare move as . . .
- ⭑ Tried to remain absolutely still
- ⭑ Warned him not to move, even though . . .
- ⭑ Watched in horror as it moved closer
- ⭑ *Hammered in her chest as . . .*
- ⭑ Only bit of him that was moving was his heart
- ⭑ Was almost deafening in the silence
- ⭑ Pounded in her temples
- ⭑ Raced through her body
- ⭑ Blasted by an explosion of terror
- ⭑ Pumped through his veins like molten lava
- ⭑ Pounded so hard it seemed about to break his ribs
- ⭑ *Held his breath*
- ⭑ Hardly dared to breathe in case he was discovered
- ⭑ Stifled a gasp
- ⭑ Choked off his breath

- Swallowed hard
- Breathed heavily
- Gulped for air
- Made her wince and tremble
- Kept his voice low
- Dropped to an urgent whisper
- Whispered in a tight, choked voice
- Clutched his hand to his mouth
- Stopped himself screaming out
- Choked back the bile that rose in her throat
- *Clenched her teeth so hard her jaw ached*
- Moved her lips silently in prayer
- *Closed her eyes*
- Peeped round the . . .
- Squeezed them shut and blinked rapidly
- Strained to pierce the darkness
- Darted wildly from side to side
- *Started to shake*
- Shaking with terror and dread
- Shook from the effort of holding herself still
- *Collected on his forehead*
- Trickled down the side of his nose into his eyes
- Panic flooded her face
- *Clasped her hands in her lap*

SENTENCES

He lingered in the shadows, motionless, alert and ready to move quickly.

She shook from the effort of holding herself still until it passed.

Every nerve in his body warned him not to move, even though his arm was shaking and pins and needles prickled painfully in his ankle.

Kitty was shaking with terror and dread that at any moment it would glance in her direction and she would be discovered.

A tingling sixth sense made him look up. As he turned his head, he froze. It was standing right above him.

He could hear the hissing calls getting closer. A shiver charged down his spine like an electric shock.

She felt the fear like a coiled spring in the pit of her stomach.

She wanted to get up and run, but she knew she couldn't. She felt a rush of air as it swiped at the branches with its clawed fingers.

As the blood pounded in her temples, her brain quickened and all her senses were alert.

Her heart hammered in her chest as she heard it moving closer and closer.

The only bit of him that was moving was his heart, which pounded so hard it seemed about to break his ribs.

As he glanced back, his heart almost stopped. They were coming at him from all directions, and closing in on him.

An explosion of adrenalin raced through her body and she quickened her pace.

She started to run, not daring to look back, the sound of her breathing roaring in her ears, her pulse thumping hard. She didn't dare stop.

The sound of his own breathing was almost deafening in the silence.

She clenched her teeth so hard her jaw ached.

Clasping her hands in her lap, she moved her lips silently in prayer.

His voice dropped to an urgent whisper.

He whispered in a tight, choked voice, watching in horror as it swooped closer.

His voice was hardly more than a whisper from the shadows.

The fear of being caught choked off his breath into unsteady, rasping gasps, until he was gulping for air.

She breathed heavily, choking back the bile that rose in her throat.

He clutched his hand to his mouth to stop himself screaming out.

When she thought of what would happen if they caught her, she was blasted by an explosion of terror that made her wince and tremble, her palms sweaty, her heart racing.

His wide eyes strained to pierce the darkness, darting wildly from side to side, certain it was somewhere nearby.

Sweat had collected on his forehead and was trickling down the side of his nose into his eyes. He squeezed them shut and blinked rapidly.

Panic flooded his face as he spotted it emerging out of the shadows.

He tried to pick up his dagger, but he was so scared his fingers felt frozen, numb, clumsy.

He was unable to move, unable to run. His mouth frozen in a silent scream, his eyes wide with terror, he stood motionless as the beast towered over him.

 **20**

Defeating the creature

Lumbering, clumsy, awkward, blundering

Fierce, vicious, furious, ferocious, savage, brutal, deadly, fatal, mortal

Venomous, poisonous, toxic

Barbed, hooked, jagged, spiked

Lashing, stabbing

Reflective, shiny

Outstretched

Verbs	**Looked**, realised, warned, alerted

Watched, followed, stared, fixed, glued, shut, squeezed

Unfurled, rose, circled, hovered, beat, flapped, folded, dived, hurtled

Gusted, swirled

Reared, dipped, thrust, pawed, gored, charged, attacked

Snapped, seized, grabbed, yanked, wrenched, dragged

Opened, spat, shot, sprayed

Clipped, jarred

Weakened, staggered, flopped, toppled, crashed, sprawled

Shielded, blocked, protected

Hesitated, waited, avoided, evaded, missed

Spread, braced, readied

Retreated, stepped back, backed away, recoiled

Edged, pressed

Side-stepped, dodged, dived, threw, flung, rolled, tumbled, crouched, huddled

Leapt, sprang, launched, bounded, vaulted

Darted, danced, buzzed, twisted, turned, whirled

Prodded, poked, rammed, barged, slammed, smashed, kicked

Picked up, tossed, spun, swung, flung, released

Seized, fitted, pointed, aimed, let loose, fired, flew

Blazed, sparked, crackled, exploded

Unsheathed, drew, gripped, clutched, flipped

Raised, poised, lowered, levelled, waved, swept, swished, brandished, wielded

Flicked, whipped

Lunged, slashed, lashed

Cut, stabbed, hacked, chopped, shoved, plunged

Hit, struck, speared, hammered, landed, lodged

Pierced, pricked, gashed, speared, impaled, skewered, severed

PHRASES – NOUNS AND ADJECTIVES

- At the very last moment
- Almost at once
- Too late
- At every movement
- *With deadly accuracy*
- With a thud
- Quick as lightning
- Like a buzzing wasp
- *In front of his face*
- Inches from his face
- *In the centre of its forehead*
- Just below the head
- At the side of the neck
- Tip of its horn
- Slavering snout
- Snapping jaws
- Savage, serrated teeth
- Blur of clashing claws and fangs
- Venomous, yellow drool
- *Golden whip*
- Blade of his spear
- Unbreakable sword
- Movement of his sword . . . a blinding blur
- *In a shower of blue sparks*
- With every deadly beat of its bat-like wings . . .
- Furious swipe of its pincers
- With one vicious jerk of her wrist . . .
- *With one final thrust . . .*

PHRASES – VERBS

- *As he looked into its eye sockets*
- Realised that it was clearly blind
- Careful to keep his movements as silent as possible
- Alerted to his presence when dead leaves rustled under his feet
- *As the shadow of the bird fell over her . . .*
- Circled above
- Folded its long, scaly wings flat against its shoulders
- Dived towards her
- Hurtled out of the sky
- Rush of air gusted towards him
- More and more dirt swirled into the cave
- *Reared up in front of her*
- Rammed its head into the entrance
- Dipped its head, gored the ground, charged
- Thrust the single spiral horn in the middle of its forehead at . . .
- Came at her in a blur of claws and fangs
- Came down to bite through his flesh
- Stinger jabbed into his shield
- Felt the barbed sting strike off the wood
- Sprayed the surface with venom
- *Hesitated a moment*
- Narrowly avoided the lashing whip of its tail
- Evaded its claws
- Evaded the venomous spines that shot from its legs
- Twice it had come close to touching him
- *Jaws snapped a hair's breadth from his leg*
- Thrust centimetres from his face
- Raked down either side of his head
- Slashed at his head
- Plunged towards his outstretched arm
- Snapped where his arm had been just seconds before
- *Seized her ankle*
- Dragged her closer to its gnashing teeth
- *Clipped his side*
- Jarred his arm painfully
- Weakened his grip
- Sent him crashing to the floor
- Hit it with such force, he staggered back
- *Crouched behind his shield*
- Lifted his shield to block the blow
- Held up his reflective shield
- *Watched the gorgon moving towards him*

- ★ Each time the gorgon changed direction . . .
- ★ Followed her movements with his shield
- ★ Protected his eyes from looking directly at her
- ★ *Watched as it dived directly at him*
- ★ Watched, horror-struck as . . .
- ★ Eyes firmly fixed on the roaring beast
- ★ Squeezed his eyes shut
- ★ *Cowered down*
- ★ Wrapped his arms over his head
- ★ *Leapt sideways*
- ★ Threw himself aside
- ★ Sprang aside as it pounced
- ★ Ducked as its claws sliced the air
- ★ Rolled across the ground away from . . .
- ★ Tumbled to one side
- ★ *Forced to retreat*
- ★ Stepped back
- ★ Backed away, edging towards . . .
- ★ Jammed up against the wall
- ★ Tried to keep it at bay
- ★ Never let the lumbering creature get too close
- ★ Fought desperately to keep its massive horned bill from . . .
- ★ Snatched a flaming branch
- ★ Jabbed the flame at its head
- ★ *Quickly scrambled back on his feet*
- ★ Scurried away on his elbows
- ★ Launched himself off the ground
- ★ Leapt over the . . .
- ★ Darted from side to side
- ★ Buzzed around like a wasp
- ★ Danced out of the way of its metal tusk
- ★ Darted out of reach of its stabbing sting
- ★ Vaulted the . . . and ducked down behind it
- ★ *Spread his feet*
- ★ Wrenched his foot away
- ★ Snatched her foot away
- ★ Yanked his foot back
- ★ Raised both boots
- ★ Kicked back
- ★ Slammed both boots into . . .
- ★ *Sprang forward*
- ★ Took a quick step forward
- ★ Lunged forward
- ★ Rolled underneath the beast

- ⋆ Launched himself between its hind legs
- ⋆ *Wings sprouted from the sides of his sandals*
- ⋆ Rose on a current of air, sword poised
- ⋆ *Picked up a handful of gravel*
- ⋆ Flung it into its eyes
- ⋆ Smashed the rock into its nose
- ⋆ *Picked up a stone from the ground*
- ⋆ Spun the sling and swung with all her might
- ⋆ Swung the sling rapidly in circles around her head
- ⋆ Released the stone with a deft flick of her wrist
- ⋆ *Flicked her golden whip out in front of her*
- ⋆ *Seized an arrow*
- ⋆ Fire blazed along the tip of the arrow
- ⋆ Fitted the arrow and let it fly
- ⋆ Pointed his arrow with deadly accuracy
- ⋆ Fired an arrow
- ⋆ Released the arrow
- ⋆ Let loose another arrow, and another
- ⋆ Flew through the air towards . . .
- ⋆ Found its mark
- ⋆ *Gripped the shaft of his spear*
- ⋆ Swung her shield from her shoulder
- ⋆ Unsheathed her dagger
- ⋆ Drew a dagger from his belt
- ⋆ Took out her dagger from her ankle strap
- ⋆ Clutched his dagger and waited in the shadows
- ⋆ *Levelled his spear at the charging beast*
- ⋆ Brandished her sword in its face
- ⋆ Bounded forward, knife raised
- ⋆ Waved her sword before her in wide sweeps
- ⋆ Sliced the air
- ⋆ Swept his sword in a low arc
- ⋆ Slashed his sword in a vicious arc
- ⋆ Lashed out with his sword
- ⋆ Lunged upwards with her sword
- ⋆ Swished back and forth with his sword
- ⋆ Cut the air into a thousand slices
- ⋆ Flipped his sword backwards
- ⋆ Gripped his sword tightly as the beast fell to the ground
- ⋆ In the time it took for him to draw back his sword . . .
- ⋆ *Smashed the beak with his shield*
- ⋆ Stabbed at its throat
- ⋆ Slashed at the underside of its body
- ⋆ Lashed at one of its talons

★ Hacked at one of its tentacles
★ Stabbed it behind the head
★ Smashed into its left eye
★ Rammed its muzzle with his shield
★ Charged, her dagger aimed at its chest
★ Drove his knife into its paw
★ Plunged deep into its thigh
★ Chopped with his scythe at the bull's head
★ Jabbed it in the ankle with his spear
★ Plunged into the beast's neck
★ Thrust her sword up into its throat
★ Lunged, shoving the blade deep into its . . .
★ Struck it between its huge fangs
★ Landed a blow on the back of the beast
★ Hammered it in the chin with the hilt of his sword
★ Hit the metal feathers, but with no effect
★ *Just missed its left eye*
★ Tore through its ruff of feathers
★ Pierced the tip of its right wing
★ Lodged in the beast's chest
★ Cut through the head of one of the writhing snakes
★ Thrust his sword into the heart of the creature
★ Aimed a slash of his sword at its side
★ Lunged at the beast's throat
★ Hacked at its leg with his sword
★ Jabbed his sword into its mouth
★ Rammed his sword between its wings
★ Struck at the back of its knee
★ Cut away some of the spikes
★ Speared it in the calf
★ Skewered the serpent with his sword
★ Severed its wing and it flopped to the ground
★ Gave the hilt a twist
★ Slid the sword into the beast's heart
★ *Creature recoiled at the touch of steel*
★ Deadly steel made contact with . . .
★ Exploded into fragments that turned to ash as they hit the ground

SENTENCES

As its tail lashed down, Kitty leapt sideways, narrowly avoiding the spikes studded along its length.

He dived to the side to evade the venomous spines that shot from its legs.

It dipped its head, pawed the ground, charged . . . thrusting the single, spiral horn in the middle of its forehead at Tom's chest. He threw himself to the side. He was too late. The tip of the horn clipped his side, sending him crashing to the ground.

It circled above, folded its long, scaly wings flat against its shoulders and dived towards her. With every beat of its huge, bat-like wings, a rush of air gusted towards her. She watched as it dived directly at her, and sprang aside at the very last moment.

It came at her in a blur of clashing claws and fangs. She ducked as its claws sliced the air in front of her face.

Tom rolled frantically across the ground away from the furious swipe of its pincers that had raked down either side of his head.

Forced to retreat, jammed up against the wall, he crouched behind his shield. He fought desperately to keep its massive horned bill from slashing at his head, but each stab of its beak jarred his arm painfully, and was weakening his grip.

She snatched her foot away as its jaws snapped a hair's breadth from her leg.

As he looked at its eye sockets, he realised that it was blind. Careful to keep his movements as silent as possible, he began backing slowly away, but dead leaves rustled under his feet and the beast froze.

Holding up his reflective shield, he watched the gorgon moving towards him. Each time she changed direction, he followed her with his shield, protecting his eyes from looking directly at her.

As he scurried back on his elbows, the slavering snout thrust inches from his face.

He cowered down, wrapped his arms over his head, squeezed his eyes shut as a powerful stream of venomous, yellow drool sprayed from its mouth.

The stinger jabbed into his shield with such force, he staggered back.

He watched, horror-struck, as its slavering jaws plunged towards his outstretched arm. He hesitated a moment, and then, his racing pulse sent a wave of adrenalin surging through his veins. He launched himself off the ground and was quickly on his feet again. Almost at once, its savage, serrated teeth snapped where his arm had been just seconds before.

Quick as lightning, she leapt aside, vaulted the wall and ducked down behind it.

As the wings sprouted from the sides of his sandals, he rose in the air, his sword poised.

With his eyes fixed on the roaring beast rearing up on its hind legs, he gripped his shield and crouched, his sword thrust out in front of him.

She darted from side to side, brandishing her sword in its face.

Like a wasp, he buzzed around, never letting the lumbering creature get too close.

Springing forward, he gripped the shaft of his spear and levelled it at the charging beast.

More and more dirt swirled into the cave with every deadly beat of its wings. Her hand slid to the dagger in her ankle strap. She slunk back into the shadows, waiting, clutching the handle.

The next moment, she bounded forward, knife raised, and slashed at the underside of its body.

With an almighty crack, she flicked her golden whip out in front of her and with another vicious flick of her wrist, she slashed at one of its tentacles.

The blade of his spear plunged deep into its thigh.

Without taking her eyes from the vile raptor, she picked up a stone from the ground. She swung the sling rapidly in circles around her head, and then, with a deft flick of her wrist, released it. She watched, holding her breath, until, with a tremendous thud, it smashed into its left eye and sent it crashing to the ground.

As it rammed its head into the entrance, she picked up a handful of gravel, flung it into its eyes and smashed its muzzle with her shield.

He backed away, edging towards the fire. When he was close enough, he lunged, snatched a flaming branch and jabbed at its head.

As it emerged in the clearing, she seized an arrow, fitted it and let it fly. The arrow flew towards its target in a shower of blue sparks, finding its mark in the centre of its forehead.

The arrow, fire blazing along the tip, flew through the air and pierced its right wing.

She let loose another arrow, and another, with deadly accuracy.

It seized her ankle and yanked, dragging her closer to its gnashing teeth. Wrenching her foot away, she leaned back and slammed both feet into its face as hard as she could.

Rolling underneath the creature, he launched himself between its hind legs, and thrust his sword up into its middle.

Darting forward, he slashed his sword in a vicious arc and sliced off one of the writhing snakes, but, in the time it took for him to draw back his sword, another had taken its place.

A searing pain jarred his arm as he struck the metal feathers, but the sword merely bounced off, with no effect. In desperation, he flipped his sword backwards and hammered it in the chin with the hilt.

He smashed the beak with his shield, and, at the same time, he stabbed his sword into its body, cutting away one of its tentacles.

Tom lunged at the beast's throat and then darted out of reach of its stabbing sting.

As the shadow of the bird fell over her, she swung her shield from her shoulder and lunged upwards with her sword.

Fire ran along the blade as he cut the air into a thousand slices, his sword a blinding blur.

Taking a quick step forward, he thrust with his spear, and skewered the serpent with the steel blade.

As the sword struck the creature's side, it recoiled. The moment the deadly steel made contact with its skin, it exploded into fragments that turned to ash as they hit the ground.

With one final thrust, he slid his sword into the beast's heart.

Appendix

Planning a myth or legend

1. The hero is in his ordinary world

The hero is in his own world that is considered to be ordinary and uneventful. The hero is often considered to possess some ability or characteristic that makes him feel that he doesn't entirely belong to that world – his abilities set him apart from his family, friends and neighbours.

★ Why is the hero different?

2. The hero is called away from his home by a discovery, event or danger

The challenge or adventure is revealed to the hero. Quests don't happen in everyday life. Heroes have to leave their ordinary life and home, family and friends to embark on their quest. They may at first be reluctant to accept the quest, but agree eventually, perhaps as a result of the discovery of a mystical object or that their world is in danger from a rival kingdom, from an evil knight or from a hideous creature.

The hero finds out about the new setting where the story is to take place.

★ Describe the event that gets the hero involved in the adventure.

3. Hero travels to the location

Describe the journey.

★ Does he meet someone who may go on the journey, give advice or give him something to complete the quest, for example, an object with magical powers, a piece of valuable wisdom as to how to defeat the villain?
★ Does he find useful clues?

Note: As the villain could be a human or creature, for ease, the term **villain** has been used and can refer to either.

4. The adventure begins

The hero gets to the new setting, where the main adventure will take place. The new setting is either in a faraway land or very different from the original setting, for example, an underground kingdom, secret forest, ruined city, castle, mountain, cave. The setting could be full of dangers and threats, including menacing creatures, knights, warriors.

As the hero has never been there before, you need to think about:

★ What does he see, hear, smell?
★ Are there any dangers/obstacles?
★ How does the new setting make him feel?

The hero:

★ will learn something about the villain that reveals the extent of the danger he faces.

5. A problem occurs in the setting/The hero meets the villain's allies

Dream up scenes and events where the hero is tested:

★ Storms
★ Losing his talisman.

The hero's experiences:

★ test his strength, bravery and determination.

The hero:

★ does not come face-to-face with the villain yet
★ learns more about the villain or the location of the object(s), person.

Don't just tell the reader what is happening. Describe the hero's feelings (reaction) and his interaction (movements/actions) with the setting and/or the enemy.

6. Hero is in great danger (the 'black moment')

★ The hero has successfully survived a series of tests and obstacles and has arrived at the final, supreme challenge he has journeyed to overcome.

★ The hero comes face-to-face with the villain. Imagine how and where the hero and villain meet.

★ Either the villain finds the hero, or the hero has found the enemy's location.

★ Describe the route the hero takes through the setting.

★ Include lots of action.

★ Describe the hero's fear/nervousness.

★ Build the suspense and atmosphere before they meet by including sounds and shadows.

★ Ask the readers questions so that they are drawn into the story.

7. Climax – final struggle/the problem is solved

Devise a plan or find something that will help the hero to face the ultimate danger.

★ Where do they meet? Describe any barriers to entering the setting, any advantages that the setting provides for the villain.

★ How does the hero defeat the villain?

★ Does the hero have any help, for example, the special object?

★ How is he feeling?

★ Is he injured?

★ What happens to the villain?

8. Resolution – the journey home

★ The hero returns home victorious. What was the result of his completing the task? Was it a reward – for example, a kingdom, a knighthood, vast riches, saving a loved one?

★ How has the adventure changed the hero?

Plot planning sheet

What happens to get the hero involved in the adventure? *Does he discover a mystical object or that his world is in danger?*	
What does the challenge involve?	
Describe the journey and route.	
Describe the new location. *Does the hero learn anything about the villain?* *Does he meet the villain's allies?*	

How does the hero meet the villain? *Where? What happens?*	
CLIMAX The hero defeats the villain. How? Does he have help? *How does his special object help him?* What happens to the villain?	
RESOLUTION The hero returns home. What is his reward? How has he changed?	
Additional notes	

Hero planning sheet

Name Age	
Physical description: face, eyes, voice, clothes, armour Distinctive features	
What is the hero most afraid of? What is his/her weakness?	
Does the hero have any secrets, skills or unusual traits? What special object does he/she have that enhances his/her powers and skills?	
What are the hero's main interests?	

Who are the members of his/her family? What do they do? Do any of them have a secret?	
Who are his/her close friends? Will any of them help/hinder the hero? Do they have any special skills or secrets?	
What has the hero got to gain by achieving the task, overcoming the challenge? What has the hero got to lose if he/she fails? How does the hero change? What is his/her reward?	
Additional information	

Creature planning sheet

Name Type Habitat	
Appearance: Parts Size Shape Colour Covering	
Head Eyes	
Body	
Arms and legs	

Wings and tails	
Smell Sound	
Movement	
Weapons/attack	
Defeat/destruction	
Additional information	

Object planning sheet

Object	
Description	
How did the object come to be in the hero's possession?	
How does the hero discover what the object can do?	
For what purpose could the object be used? *Guidance, protection, escape, weapon*	
How and when does the hero use the object?	
Additional information	

The setting

SETTING/CHARACTER	INTERACTION	REACTION

The creature

SETTING/CHARACTER	INTERACTION	REACTION

Suspense: wind/sky

SETTING/CHARACTER	INTERACTION	REACTION

Suspense: storms

SETTING/CHARACTER	INTERACTION	REACTION

Suspense: rain

SETTING/CHARACTER	INTERACTION	REACTION

Suspense: waves and currents

SETTING/CHARACTER	INTERACTION	REACTION

Suspense: sounds, smells, touch

SETTING/CHARACTER	INTERACTION	REACTION